LOST IN TRANSLATION

LOST IN TRANSLATION

HOW MEN AND WOMEN CAN
UNDERSTAND EACH OTHER

DR. STEVE STEPHENS

MULTNOMAH
BOOKS

Lost in Translation
Published by Multnomah Books
12265 Oracle Boulevard, Suite 200
Colorado Springs, Colorado 80921
A division of Random House Inc.

ISBN 978-1-59052-706-1

Library of Congress Cataloging-in-Publication Data
Stephens, Steve.
    Lost in translation : how men and women can understand each other / Steve
Stephens.—1st ed.
        p. cm.
    ISBN 978-1-59052-706-1
    1. Man-woman relationships—Religious aspects—Christianity. 2. Sex role—Religious
aspects—Christianity. I. Title.
    BT705.8.S74 2007
    248.8'44—dc22

                                                                    2007015277

Printed in the United States of America
2007—First Edition

10 9 8 7 6 5 4 3 2 1

Special Sales
Most WaterBrook Multnomah books are available in special quantity discounts when
purchased in bulk by corporations, organizations, and special interest groups. Custom
imprinting or excerpting can also be done to fit special needs. For information, please
e-mail SpecialMarkets@WaterBrookPress.com or call 1-800-603-7051.

Other Books by Dr. Steve Stephens

The Worn Out Woman
The Walk Out Woman
The Wounded Woman
The Wounded Warrior
Blueprints for a Solid Marriage
20 Surprisingly Simple Rules and Tools series
…for a Great Marriage
…for a Great Family
…for a Great Day

Contents

ONE

Watch Your Toes!

"Men are all alike," Callie seethed.

"That's not fair," her husband, Greg, insisted. "I'm not like every other man. I'm my own person."

"But look how you act."

"Sure, I act like a guy. That's because I am a guy. That's not all bad. You fell in love with me because I'm a guy. Why is it all of a sudden a negative?"

"I guess I didn't realize what I was getting into back then." Callie gave Greg a smile that left him wondering whether she really meant what she had just said.

"Well…" Greg fished for a worthy retort. "If you're going to pick on us guys, then I can pick on women just as easily. Like, women don't make any sense. Everything has to do with how they feel. And their feelings are constantly changing. On top of that, they worry about everything. And they can't stop talking. Women drive guys nuts, but at least we're polite enough to keep our mouths shut about it."

"Polite? Did you say polite? I can't believe what I just heard." Callie's face reddened. "You don't want to get me going on the subject of men and politeness…"

Greg and Callie managed to stretch out this little altercation a full two weeks. With breaks for food and sleep.

Every couple fights. Partners disagree, they stand up for what they believe is right, and they do everything they can to prove their points. They fight about finances, sex, relatives, who does what around the house, children, and a hundred other issues that are usually pettier than any of us want to admit. I know all about fights. Tami and I have certainly had our share.

Yet what amazes me, after working with couples for over twenty-five years, is that what we *think* we're fighting about is rarely what we're really fighting about. A battle about finances might really be about security. Or interdependence. Or respect. At its heart, a fight about sex probably springs out of issues like love, communication, or connection.

And the biggest *real* issue of all? I've come to the conclusion that at least 50 percent of all fights between husbands and wives are, at their roots, about gender differences. I've also come to another conclusion: *if we could understand these differences, then maybe we wouldn't fight as much.*

That's the point of this book—to help you understand your spouse better and learn to appreciate him or her more. My intent is not to stock your bunker with ammo, reinforcing all the ways you think your spouse should change. My purpose is to improve your relationship with your husband or wife. Understanding these differences allows us to be tolerant of our partners.

I frequently hear men and women say things like:

Men	Women
"I don't understand her."	"Why don't men get it?"
"Can't she ever make up her mind?"	"Why does he act like that?"

Men	Women
"Why does she do the things she does?"	"He makes me so crazy."
"Women are so complicated."	"He makes me so angry."
"She is totally random!"	"They just don't make any sense."
"What in the world does she want?"	"I'll never figure him out."

Yet men understand how men think, and women understand how women think. The bottom line is that gender relations are truly a cross-cultural experience. Men and women think, feel, and communicate differently. Sometimes *a whole lot* differently. We "speak" different languages.

But does that mean we can never understand each other? NO! There's hope! We can learn to *translate* each other's language. And when we do, we learn that the opposite sex is a lot less complicated and mysterious than we thought.

You've been engaged in the age-old battle of the sexes. It's time to call a truce. Talks can begin. You'll need to consciously set aside old offenses…and new ones. Because I assure you, honesty about gender differences *will* offend you. That's why I can safely predict that this book is bound to tick you off.

Whenever somebody writes about the differences between men and women, the author is guaranteed to step on someone's toes. So put on your steel-toed boots (or your steel-toed pumps). Men will think I side too much with women—I, a caring, compassionate psychologist who has listened to the hurts and frustrations of countless women. Women, on the other hand, will insist that I side with men. After all, I *am* one; what more is there to say? How can I sleep at night? Well, if I frustrate men and women equally, I figure I'm doing a good job.

And speaking of frustrations, here's another warning. To write about gender differences, one must write in generalities. You'll see me constantly using words like *often*, *tends*, *frequently*, *commonly*, *usually*, *may*, *might*, *most*, and *many*. This is my way of covering myself, since much of what I say might not be totally true of you. For example, verbal, relational men are going to feel as if I'm saying they're feminine, while competitive, nonemotional women will think I'm saying they're masculine. This is *not* what I'm saying.

The differences are real. And they're true about men and women *in general*. But no trait is totally characteristic of all men or all women. We are all individuals; there is no cookie-cutter mold determining what a man or a woman is. Many factors besides gender—factors such as individual genetics, birth order, role models, early childhood experience, learning, and personality—interact to make each of us incredibly unique.

My mom was a great mechanic. My dad was not mechanical in the least. I grew up knowing that if I needed help with my car, I should go to Mom. Dad might try to fix it, but he was as likely as not to make it worse.

Enter Tami. And marriage. The garbage disposal breaks. Whom do I ask to fix it? Why, Tami, of course. But Tami comes from a foreign land—the land where dads are the fixers. A concept that baffled me. Our experiences had shaped our expectations—part of who we were. And in that respect, I was an exception to the male rule.

So let me affirm clearly from the outset: there is *nothing* wrong with you if you don't match up exactly with the typical characteristics of your gender. I visit often with couples who have reversed gender roles in certain areas. Many couples are made up of compassionate men and competitive women. Or women with the stronger sex drive. Or men who are more verbal. These couples find ways to compensate, and their atypical differences have no more impact on their relationship than the typical differences do on typical couples.

Now, a lot of people use differences as an excuse to stubbornly dig in their heels and say, "This is who I am. I can't change. So you'd better just accept it." Yes, acceptance is important, but a healthy relationship also means give and take by both partners (preferably more give than take). Neither women nor men should be expected to make all the changes. In most situations, both need to shift. But sometimes men need to take the bigger steps—like learning to listen and share their hearts more. And sometimes women are called on to change more— maybe becoming more sensitive to their husbands' sexual needs or showing greater respect. (Oops! Did I just step on any toes?)

To all whom I will offend or misrepresent in the following pages…I'm sorry. I empathize with the difficulties of learning a new language. But I rejoice in the hope that, as you learn, God will answer my prayer—that the following short chapters will bring you and your spouse closer together in a marriage that is becoming ever

- richer,
- sweeter,
- and more exciting.

Because you're different.

CHAPTER SUMMARY

One of the ways we can improve our marriages is by gaining understanding about the opposite gender. But no one perfectly fits all of his or her gender's typical traits.

1. In what ways are most men alike?
2. In what ways are most women alike?
3. How are each of you different from the norm for men and women?

TWO

The Norwegyptian Merger

love my wife.

I love being married.

Yet sometimes Tami drives me crazy.

We've been married more than twenty-three years, and I'm still amazed at how much I *don't* understand about this relationship. Her words and actions often baffle me. They make no sense. And just as often, my words and actions are equally nonsensical to her.

And yet, wonder of wonders, Tami tells me that our relationship gets better every year. Of course, during that first difficult year, there wasn't much choice but to improve. Otherwise we might not be married today. I was a psychologist and thought, naturally, that I knew all about relationships. When we got married, I thought everything would be perfect. After all, we'd known each other a long time, we had fun together, we were both good people, and most importantly, we were in love. Wasn't that the recipe for a match made in heaven?

Apparently not.

After a month or two of marriage, I came home from work one day to find Tami locked in the bathroom crying. Bringing to bear all my professional and husbandly concern, I knocked on the door and asked her what was wrong.

"I don't know," came the reply.

"But something must be wrong," I said as gently as I knew how.

"I don't know!" She started sobbing even harder.

"Why don't you let me in?"

"No. I don't want you to see me crying."

"It's okay," I said patiently. "I've seen you cry before."

"But I'm ugly when I cry."

"Everybody is ugly when they cry." I sat down outside the door.

"See? You think I'm ugly when I cry."

Idiot! I berated myself. To her: "No, I don't. I just want to figure out why you're so upset."

"I'm just upset."

"But there must be a reason."

"I can't do anything right."

"There are plenty of things you do right," I said, thinking we were finally getting to the bottom of this.

"You're just saying that."

"No, I really mean it."

"If you really meant it, you'd have told me that before." A pause. A sob. "Why is it you only compliment me when I'm upset or you want sex?"

"That's not true." My defenses suddenly reared up. *How in the world did we get from her doing nothing right to sex?*

"Yes, it is." I could hear her determination through the door. "If it's not true, give some examples."

"Well, I can't think of any right now."

"See? I told you I was right."

I don't know how much longer the conversation went on, but the longer it went, the more confused I became. Everything I said seemed to dig me deeper into a hole, and I couldn't climb out. I still didn't know why she was so upset. I didn't even understand what we were arguing about.

It's a universal reality. Men and women are so different that we frequently drive each other to frustration and confusion. We don't do it on purpose; we just do it. Over the past twenty-five years, as I've worked with thousands of couples, I've come to realize that a large portion of marriage problems are because men and women...

- see differently.
- hear differently.
- think differently.
- feel differently.
- communicate differently.
- relate to life differently.

Men and women are as different as night and day. Both genders have their advantages and disadvantages, their strengths and weaknesses. It's not that one is right and the other wrong. But in our hearts we often believe that. Tami once asked me why I was so persistent when we fought. I confidently asserted that I only got into arguments when I knew I was absolutely right.

Yeah, right. I had fallen into an all-too-common trap, and over the years Tami has often "rescued" me from it by proving me wrong. So many times, in fact, that I've learned to fight a little less persistently, a little more tentatively and humbly.

In the musical *My Fair Lady*, Professor Higgins speaks for billions of men: "Why can't a woman be more like a man?" With the mere transposition of two words we can form the question that just as many women have asked: "Why can't a man be more like a woman?" In spite of the predictable confusion, God in His infinite wisdom created us different.

The first chapter of the first book of the Bible says, "So God created man in his own image, in the image of God he created him; male and female he created them" (Genesis 1:27). I can't count the times that as I listen to couples in my office, I stop them midsentence and say something like, "There he goes again, thinking like a man" or "She's way too much like a woman." The couple chuckles, but they get the point. When they get stuck, I frequently ask partners to say, "I'm sorry, I'm being a man" or "I'm sorry, I'm being a woman."

Men and women grow up in different worlds and speak different languages. It's similar to the difficulty of a person who grew up in Norway, speaking Norwegian, trying to communicate with someone who grew up in Egypt, speaking Egyptian. Meanings, intentions, understanding—it's so easy for them to get lost in translation. Men and women, by their very natures and training, start out with built-in incompatibilities. Each has radically different goals, emotional needs, environmental conditioning, and ways of looking at the world. It's good to remember these facts of life.

Couples in troubled marriages continually complain and try to change each other. Couples with the best marriages learn how to understand and be sensitive to their differences.

So don't fight the differences. Work with them. In this way affirm each other, and you'll avoid a lot of unnecessary conflicts and frustrations. Then you can enjoy each other—laugh, relax, have fun, work together. Marriage can become all it was meant to be. It will never be perfect, but hopefully it will get better every year.

I know what I'm talking about. Tami hasn't locked herself in the bathroom, crying uncontrollably, for at least a year or two.

CHAPTER SUMMARY

Gender differences can drive both husband and wife crazy. But *it is possible* to turn these differences into strengths.

1. What differences between the two of you frustrate you most?
2. What differences do you think might frustrate your spouse the most?
3. How has a gender difference recently escalated into a conflict? How could you have handled it better?

THREE

The Problem with Pollyanna

E verybody has expectations.

Most people who get married have positive expectations; otherwise they wouldn't marry. They fall in love, tie the knot, and believe they will live happily ever after.

Like Jerry and Samantha. Their honeymoon was wonderful. Jerry was patient and thoughtful and incredibly romantic. He complimented Samantha constantly and held her hand whenever they were out in public. Samantha glowed with the ecstasy of a dream come true. She couldn't have been happier.

Then the honeymoon ended. Jerry and Samantha went back to work; finances grew tight; stress increased. Jerry became more impatient and less romantic. He was still a nice guy, but he was no longer the knight in shining armor. Samantha grew frustrated, then disappointed, then depressed. At first Jerry didn't notice. When he did, he withdrew; he didn't know what else to do. Lonely woman, confused man.

Samantha complained to a good friend, "This isn't what I expected. I feel cheated and deceived." Six months later she filed for divorce.

———————

Women tend to have higher expectations of marriage than most men. They plan fantasy weddings from the time they're young girls. The picture-perfect ceremony—everything beautifully orchestrated—is supposed to be the prelude to a picture-perfect marriage. Women dream of a relationship with more communication, togetherness, kindness, courtesy, and romance than most men consider practical or even possible.

"Women want the fairy tale," wrote the popular novelist Nicholas Sparks. Women hold idealized expectations. Men, on the other hand, are more realistic. One woman told me, "They have low expectations. Keep them well fed, sexually satisfied, and busy. Then they will tolerate just about anything." I know this is a major oversimplification, but my point is that men are more pragmatic than women. Men don't expect things to go smoothly.

Am I right, guys? Is life perfect? Is marriage a fairy tale? Does this imperfect reality upset you? Or do you just accept it as "the way it is"? (And ladies, does that series of questions upset you?)

Men know that marriage may include wonderful, magical, precious moments, but these can easily fade. Life is sometimes hard and at times downright miserable.

Now don't get me wrong. I think marriage is great, and I'm glad I got married. It's one of the best things I've ever done. But it's far from perfect. Those who are married tend to be healthier, wealthier, and happier than those who aren't. Yet sometimes people build up marriage to be more wonderful than it is. Expectations can get people into trouble. If I think a friend is going to give me a thousand dollars and he only gives me a hundred, I might become angry and disappointed. But it's still a generous gift, and I'm better off than before I got the hundred dollars. Or am I?

Unrealistic expectations can make one bitter or depressed. It can destroy what people have because they can't get their eyes off what might have been. I have found that unrealistic expectations is one of the top reasons for marital dissatisfaction. Every day I hear statements like these:

"Things didn't work out the way I thought they would."

"Marriage isn't all it's cracked up to be."

"He's no knight in shining armor."

"She's not as fun or patient or tolerant as she used to be."

These issues are not the problem—they're just reality. Yet most couples have a hard time negotiating the disconnect between expectations and reality. They are unable (or possibly unwilling) to give up their unrealistic expectations and do what they can to convert their reasonable expectations into reality. Maybe the problem isn't the marriage. Maybe the problem is that many of us have formed fantasies about marriage that have never been true and will never be possible. The reality is that when you put two imperfect people together, you will have an imperfect relationship. Add a little stress to the mix, and things can get tough. On top of this, add disappointment because things aren't the way you thought they'd be, and you have a setup for disaster.

Here are some of the most common unrealistic expectations couples struggle with. They might seem positive or reasonable, but they just aren't true.

Marriage will be easy. The reality is that a good marriage is very hard work. That's just the way it is. It doesn't come naturally, and it's full of challenges. The harder you work at marriage, the better it will be.

Marriage will be fun. Every marriage can have its share of fun if you have a positive and optimistic attitude. But it will also be full of frustrations, annoyances, hurts, and disappointments. And what fun you do have must be created intentionally.

Marriage will fulfill me. Marriage by itself will not make you happy, solve all your problems, or give your life meaning. In fact, at times it will drain you and complicate your life. Marriage is not a cure-all, but it can be wonderfully fulfilling.

Marriage will be fair. Life is not fair, and neither is marriage. There will be times you are misunderstood, unappreciated, taken for granted, overworked, and pushed to the limit. At times your spouse will get away with murder, and nothing will go your way. But with patience, things often have a way of turning around.

Love conquers all. If by "love" you mean the feeling, I guarantee that will come and go. The many demands of everyday life tarnish the romance. Over time, traits like commitment, loyalty, generosity, and sacrifice become more important than emotional love. If your hope for a successful marriage is based on feeling "in love," you'll soon run out of steam.

It can't happen to us. You might think, *We're good people—Christians, smart, hard-working, caring...* But nobody is immune to difficulties or tragedies. Affairs, abuse, sickness, financial crisis, dishonesty, addictions, boredom, midlife crisis, and even divorce can happen to the best of people. Protect yourself from the worst by doing all you can to build the strongest marriage possible.

False expectations are trouble. But true expectations—honestly facing the good, the bad, and the frustrating—help you prepare to enjoy what you have rather than resenting what you don't have.

Your marriage can be positive and strongly committed without being perfect. Tami and I both have strong personalities; neither of us is afraid to stand toe-to-toe with the other. Sometimes I think she is totally wrong, and sometimes she thinks I am totally wrong. But we love each other. In fact, one of the reasons I love and appreciate her is because she's not perfect.

Perfect marriages make me nervous. In part because I think somebody's lying, and in part because I'd hate to try to live up to that expectation. If Tami were perfect, then she wouldn't be satisfied with me. We don't have a flawless marriage, but it's just right for me. When all is said and done, I love Tami just the way she is.

Maybe love does conquer all.

At least every once in a while.

CHAPTER SUMMARY

We all start with idealistic expectations for our marriages. By adjusting to realistic expectations, we can begin to be more thankful for what we have.

1. How have your expectations about marriage led to disappointment?
2. Which one of you has the highest expectations about your relationship?
3. Which of the six expectations on pages 14–15 have you fallen into? In what ways were they true or false?

FOUR

He Wants, She Wants

W hy can't he just give me what I need?" Andrea asked. "It's not that hard."

"Why can't she relax and let it go?" Dale complained. "Everything doesn't have to be such a big deal."

Andrea wanted more quality time.

Dale wanted more sex.

Andrea wanted sit-down meals.

Dale wanted to go out to a movie.

Andrea wanted to invite friends over.

Dale wanted to work in the yard.

They both had expectations. Their expectations clashed. And the results weren't pretty.

No marriage is perfect, and no spouse is perfect. Yet most people hold a fantasy picture of what their spouse should be like. It's a pleasant fantasy, but it's probably based more on romantic movies, books, love songs, wishful thinking, and the flush of first love than on reality.

One of my college professors, Grant Howard, wrote: "We have a picture of the perfect partner, but we marry an imperfect person. Then we have two options. Tear up the picture and accept the person, or tear up the person and accept the picture." I've met too many people who still hold their whimsical picture of a perfect spouse in their heart. Every time they pull it out and compare it to their partner, they look away disappointed with what they have.

It's time to get real.

Men and women usually have their own unique sets of unrealistic expectations. Here are some of hers:

1. **He will know my needs.**

    But why should he? He doesn't think like you and never will. Give the guy a break. If you need something, tell him. Don't beat around the bush; just tell him.

2. **He will meet all my needs.**

    It won't happen! Not even if you tell him what you need. But he can meet some of them. Look to God, friends, and family to meet the rest.

3. **He will talk to me more.**

    Sure, he can try harder and probably should. But remember, he doesn't feel as comfortable talking as you do, especially about emotions, difficulties, and relationships.

4. **He will live up to his potential.**

    Women have a wonderful ability to see the potential in men. That's part of the reason you married him. Encourage him, but realize that he might never reach all the goals you think he could.

5. **He will not be like other guys.**

    Of course he will. He need not be crude, rude, or crass. But do you really want him to be like a woman? Guys are guys.

Within limits, there's nothing wrong with these normal everyday expectations. But you'll find only unhappiness if you cling to them. Let go of the ones with which you're shackling your husband. And if any of them do come true, celebrate!

Now men also have their own set of unrealistic expectations. His are neither better nor worse than hers. Both sets are equally unrealistic, unreasonable, and unfair.

1. **She will always tell me what she needs.**

   Sure, she's a great communicator, but she still needs you to give her time, talk, and reassurance without her having to ask.

2. **She will be less verbal and emotional.**

   This is where she lives. Don't shut her down. Let her talk; you listen. Let her emote; you comfort and affirm.

3. **She will understand me.**

   You're so different from her; how can she understand unless you talk to her? Tell her what's on your mind and heart. It won't kill you.

4. **She will be tough and not fall apart.**

   You think you want her to be a man? Let her be feminine. You be the tough one. Come alongside her and help her when she falls apart.

5. **She will know how much I love her.**

   Yes, you show love by working hard. But she needs more. She needs dates and flowers and cards. She needs you to say "I love you" when you aren't in the bedroom.

Expectations aren't all bad. But they can set us up for disappointment. They can trap individuals in an egocentric perspective where a spouse is supposed to "meet my needs" and "see things my way" and "do things my way." Expectations keep individuals in a state of immaturity where they don't face the reality of marriage or the inevitability of differences. Immaturity clings to what it wants and throws tantrums when it doesn't get it.

In contrast, maturity knows that, no matter how one thinks or believes life *should* be, every couple must live in reality. Healthy couples put aside their false expectations. They generously accept their differences. They honor, appreciate, and celebrate their partner's otherness, even when it dashes their expectations.

Unmet expectations lead to resentment, and resentment is the killer of relationships. Resentment is cold and bitter. It points the blaming finger and spits the accusation: "You didn't treat me like I deserved." Resentment can't—or won't—see anyone else's perspective.

But resentment can be remedied. *Flexibility* lets go of unrealistic and unmet expectations. Someone once said, "The world is cruel to the rigid, but kind to the flexible." *Forgiveness* refuses to hold on to the hurt and disappointment; it moves on. It's one of the greatest gifts you can give your spouse—and yourself. And *favor* embraces one's partner with love and compassion. With these, your marriage can flourish.

Andrea cried and felt deceived when her dreams about marriage didn't come true. She could hardly believe that Dale would act like he did. Dale was shocked that his beloved bride could be so demanding and petty. Both withdrew into their hurt and silence. They each believed they were right, and they had plenty of reasons to justify their own positions. To further entrench them against each other, they both found friends or relatives who took sides and were appalled at the selfishness and insensitivity of the other partner. Over the next year their relationship grew distant and icy.

A friend noticed what was going on and asked them both out to dinner. "What in the world are you two doing?" he asked. "You both dig in your heels and blame the other. But I think you're both wrong. Grow up and forgive each other. I know you both love each other, so why are you being so silly?"

Andrea and Dale were shocked at their friend's confrontation. But they realized that maybe it was exactly what they needed. Their marriage wasn't what either had expected, but it had some wonderful aspects. They agreed to start over without their individual agendas and expectations. Soon the distance faded; the ice melted. They still have moments of disappointment, but they refuse to hold on to them. As Dale told me not long ago, "Expectations take you nowhere, but forgiveness and an other-focused attitude can take you anywhere you want."

"It can even take you to Hawaii," Andrea chimed in with a big grin. "Because that's where we're headed next Saturday, and I can hardly wait."

CHAPTER SUMMARY

Men and women tend to have different expectations of each other. If we're not careful, they can lead to resentment.

1. In what ways are your expectations about marriage different from your spouse's?
2. Which of the expectations on pages 18–19 did each of you hold when you were first married?
3. What types of expectations do you still have of each other?
4. Does your spouse believe that your expectations are fair?

It's a Good Thing *Someone* Knows the Rules

M en are good at a lot of things. But when it comes to relationships, most men are clueless.

That's one reason why we men should celebrate our oh-so-different wives! Not only do they have a clue or two about relationships, but they're the ones who do the most work to keep our relationships intact and on track.

Women are relationship oriented; men are more task oriented. Women tend to be tender, gentle, soft, compassionate, understanding, and caring. When my kids get hurt, they want their mother. But when they want to problem-solve, they usually come to me.

Women love to relate. They look for every opportunity to strengthen, nurture, protect, deepen, and improve their relationships—especially with their husbands. Women know that the proper maintenance of a healthy relationship is guided by The Rules.

It's because of The Rules that Rachel finds Mondays so hard.

Take last Monday, for example. Henry turned off the alarm without opening his eyes. He wandered into the shower and stood motionless, waiting for the hot steam to pull him into a wide-awake world. It didn't work.

Twenty minutes later he left for the office without saying a word to Rachel. The day sped by with no phone call to or connection with his wife. When he returned home, Henry was so preoccupied by a project at work that he...

- didn't ask Rachel about her day.
- didn't kiss her hello.
- didn't notice her new blouse.
- didn't answer her questions.
- hardly acknowledged her existence.

Henry headed straight for his recliner, flipped on the TV, and watched the news. He opened the mail and complained about how much Rachel had charged on the Visa. He ate dinner, loudly voicing his hatred for leftovers. Then he worked late into the evening.

Rachel went to bed alone. As she stared at the ceiling, she began to calculate how many relationship rules Henry had broken that day.

The Rules are so obvious to most women that it is hard for them to believe that men don't know them. Here's the truth: not only do men not know The Rules—most men don't even know they *exist*. Wives think their husbands are being rude, stubborn, uncaring, or selfish. But this isn't true. Well, not most of the time. Men are just being clueless.

It's a good thing *someone* knows The Rules, or else all our relationships would die of thirst and neglect. Women realize that relationships are fragile things, like plants. If they're not carefully tended—watered, fertilized, placed in the sunshine, and periodically pruned—they will eventually wither and die.

Henry shows his love by working hard and providing for his family. That's a good thing. Rachel shows her love by taking care of the relationship—also very important. She talks about the relationship, reads about the relationship, thinks about the relationship, and worries about the relationship—all of which reinforce basic relationship rules she has known since she was young.

The Rules are seldom verbalized in any systematic way. Why should they be? Women assume they're obvious reflections of reality. So I have taken active steps to learn The Rules.

Over the past five years, I've asked over a thousand women what exactly The Rules are. They responded exuberantly, and I scribbled their thoughts as quickly as I could. I was overwhelmed by the sheer number of rules. But I was also surprised by the amazing similarities in the lists, regardless of age, education, socioeconomic status, faith, or marital history. Then I took the most common rules and asked thirty-two married women I trust and respect to prioritize the list. Here is my compilation of all this research, beginning with the most important rules:

1. Communicate.
2. Listen carefully.
3. Make your spouse a priority.
4. Watch your attitude.
5. Relax and have fun with each other.
6. Do the little things.
7. Say "I love you" frequently.
8. Compliment daily.
9. Fight fair.
10. Be romantic.
11. Go on dates together.
12. Share.
13. Mind your manners.
14. Celebrate birthdays and anniversaries in a big way.
15. Watch less TV.

Men have a much harder time articulating The Rules. They feel more comfortable talking about occupations, cars, sports, or politics—almost anything other than relationships. In fact, few things freak out a husband more than when his wife says, "Honey, I think we need to talk about our relationship." Yes, guys, I know this makes you nervous, but talking about the relationship is a good thing. It's one way you and your wife can explore The Rules; together you can open up the owner's manual for marriage.

The female's finely tuned relationship receptors not only pick up on The Rules—they are also tuned in to emotions. Rachel can identify how she feels about something faster and more accurately than Henry. Henry has just as many feelings as Rachel, but he, like most men, is less open and honest about them. He processes his feelings internally; she talks them out.

Men have a greater ability to ignore their emotions, so they appear to be (and often truly are) out of touch with what they're feeling. Men can suppress uncomfortable emotions, which might make them feel calmer but can also allow negative emotions to grow below the surface.

But thank God for Rachel's radar. She frequently identifies Henry's emotions before he does. Henry doesn't like when other people—especially his wife—tell him how he feels. But he's starting to realize that she can sometimes help him resolve inner tensions he didn't know he had. Especially when she respectfully and politely brings up the subject by asking, "Do you feel this?" or "It looks like you might be feeling that?" He finds her input easier to swallow when she *asks* him, rather than tells him.

If a wife senses that her husband is angry, depressed, stressed, hurt, tired, or frustrated, she is probably right. So, men, try not to deny or be defensive about such observations. Ask yourself, *Could she be right? Is there any truth, even the tiniest amount, to what she's saying?* By means of a woman's insight, a couple can gain an accurate pulse on the marriage's health.

When couples come to my office for the first time, I frequently ask each spouse separately, "How is your marriage?" The husband usually says, "Everything is fine." The wife usually tells me, "Things are not going well." Then she proceeds to give me a list of her concerns and potential danger signs. As I evaluate the relationship over the next couple of sessions, I find that the wife is almost always right. Men either minimize or fail to recognize the warning signs that women spot much more readily.

So, as an aid to men, and as a review of what you ladies already know, let me run through a few diagnostic questions you should ask yourselves. If you answer yes to any of these, your marriage might need help.

- Do you enjoy spending time with others more than with your spouse?
- Has it been a month or more since you've had sexual relations?
- Are you easily distracted or bored when your mate is talking?
- Do you look for excuses to stay away from home?
- Are you impatient or easily irritated with your partner?
- Has it been a month or more since you've gone out alone with your spouse?
- Have you recently had any thoughts of divorce or separation?
- Do you think your mate doesn't understand you?
- Has there been a loss of trust or respect?
- Are you negative, sarcastic, or critical toward each other?
- Do you communicate less now than one year ago?
- Have you stopped laughing and having fun together?
- Do you argue about the same issue over and over again?
- Is either of you less than totally honest with the other?
- Do you feel unappreciated or unloved by your spouse?
- Has it been three months or more since you've given your mate a gift?
- Is it hard for you to forgive your partner?
- Do you run out of things to talk about when you're together?
- Is it difficult to think of compliments for your mate?

Guys, let's try to appreciate it more when our wives' relational radar kicks in. They have the barometers that can help us see a storm coming.

Yes, our wives are constantly coaxing us into being more relational. But face it: the few things they want from us are nothing compared to the work they do. Women are constantly looking for ways to improve the marriage. They plan dates at romantic restaurants, buy relationship books and leave them on our nightstands, cuddle up next to us for a meaningful conversation, wear provocative night wear in a candlelit bedroom. Women try hard. And we men need to value all their efforts.

I know, her attempts sometimes feel like an invasion of your space, a distraction from your agenda. She may draw you into a conversation that ends up being longer and more personal than you're comfortable with. But why does she do all these things? Because she loves you. When she stops trying? That's when you should start worrying.

CHAPTER SUMMARY

Women are generally more aware than men of relational "rules," of his and her true emotions, and of trouble spots in the marriage. Men should learn to value their wives' relational radar.

1. What are some of the most important relationship rules the two of you have?
2. How would each of you separately prioritize the fifteen rules on page 24?
3. Which rules do you struggle with most? Which rules does your spouse struggle with most?

SIX

The Point System

M en are graded every day.

As they walk through life, most men are completely unaware of the multitude of actions (and inactions) that impact their wives' hearts. Their wives are very aware; they keep track. Everything a man does gets a positive, negative, or neutral rating. Men forget a lot of the day's details; women don't. Each evening a woman consciously or subconsciously tallies up her husband's score for the day and stores it away in her memory. If he has earned more positive points than negative, she feels good about the relationship. But if he has earned more negative points, she's unhappy with him and the relationship.

It's a simple system. Daily points are added together for weekly, monthly, and yearly totals. And the system's actually valuable to the relationship. It helps a woman know whether the relationship is positive or negative and whether it's improving or declining. Men cruise along, obliviously assuming all is well. When the bottom drops out and she goes to pieces, he proclaims *honestly* that he never saw it coming. It was probably coming for months. Maybe years. He just wasn't tracking the point tally.

During the first seven months of our marriage, I lost more points than I gained. At the time I wasn't sure what I was doing wrong, but I knew that Tami was more moody, withdrawn, and tearful than normal. She was still kind and loving, but not as carefree as she had once been. I tried to do nice things for her. But apparently my accumulation of negatives was slowly outweighing my positives.

Then one day the problem came clear to me: *Tami didn't like our house.*

I had bought our 1904 bungalow several years before we started dating. To Tami it was *my* house, not *our* house. In those first seven months she made numerous complaints about the house. It was too far from our friends. It smelled musty. Its stairs were too steep. It got too hot in the summer. It didn't have much of a yard. It didn't feel safe. And more. Since I didn't see any remedies, I dismissed her complaints with, "Don't worry; you'll get used to the house." (This alone probably cost me at least a thousand points.)

Then I got it! On a hot summer afternoon I went to Tami and asked, "Would you like to sell this house and find one that you feel totally comfortable with?"

Suddenly Tami felt heard. She jumped up and down, gave me a huge hug, and said, "That would be wonderful!" The next seven months went much better. Together we built *our* new house, much closer to her friends and family. Together we looked at plans, property, plumbing fixtures, carpet samples, paint, and a lot more. Instead of just doing it my way, I invited her opinions and her preferences. As I learned to listen better, I regained all the points I'd lost. With plenty more to spare. (Could you use a few of my extras?) And it's The Point System that saved me. If I hadn't picked up on Tami's unhappiness and figured out that I was deep in negative territory, I never would have known to take such important action on her behalf.

Since then we've had our ups and downs. I try to accumulate as many positive points as possible. But to do this, I must be aware of what draws Tami closer to me and what pushes her away. Words in particular have incredible power to do both. Here are several plus-point statements:

- "I love you."
- "I was wrong."
- "Good job!"
- "What would you like?"
- "You are wonderful."
- "Thank you."
- "Let me just listen."
- "I missed you today."
- "What can I do to help?"

And here are a few of the words that are guaranteed to lose points:

- "I told you so."
- "I can do whatever I like."
- "What's your problem?"
- "Can't you be more responsible?"
- "You're always in a bad mood."
- "Can't you do anything right?"
- "I can't do anything to please you."
- "You're impossible."
- "It's your fault."

Actions and attitudes can win or lose points too. When men are helpful, attentive, generous, protective, patient, and caring, they get points. The same when they exhibit a positive attitude that is kind, encouraging, respectful, and loving.

But let me give you the top-ten list of ways men can lose points big time, sometimes without even knowing it:

1. angry outbursts
2. criticalness
3. selfishness
4. neglect
5. overcontrol
6. dishonesty
7. demands
8. irresponsibility
9. meanness
10. insensitivity

And, of course, a man loses points for not following The Rules (see chapter 5). "But I don't know The Rules," he protests. Unfortunately, this defense doesn't fly with his wife. In her mind, ignorance is never an excuse.

Men may ignore The Point System, deny it, resist it, and get ticked off by it. But none of that stops the grading. Men's preference on the issue is irrelevant. Points are a reality that's here to stay. So we can stubbornly choose to stumble around in the dark, or we can get our wives to help us.

I choose to get all the help I can. Tami helps me by constantly giving me feedback. She says things like, "You're making points," "That was worth a lot of points," or "You just lost points, mister." This helps me either stay on the right path or get back on it if I've gone astray. I stray more often than I like to admit.

Now, women are not rigid enforcers of The Point System. Most are willing to give grace in the event of a special difficulty, a trauma, or just a bad day. But if a string of exceptions builds into a pattern, women quickly withdraw their grace.

All that most women want is a healthy relationship where they feel loved, not taken advantage of. Bottom line, that's what The Point System is all about.

Men who truly love their wives and are willing to show it regularly have nothing to fear. Too much time spent in negative habits or attitudes digs a pit that's often hard to climb out of.

But, guys, take courage. Don't give up.

You can build a great marriage.

You can rekindle the romance.

You can win back her heart.

You can do it.

Just check the scoreboard every now and then.

CHAPTER SUMMARY

Women are designed to keep tallies of positive or negative points for everything their husbands do. Men can best love their wives if both partners communicate about The Point System.

1. Men, what sorts of things cause you to gain or lose points with your wife?
2. Women, what are the most outstanding point gainers and losers your husband does?
3. What's the point balance between you now? Is it positive or negative? By a lot or a little? (Give specific examples why.)

SEVEN

Sponges and Turtles

McKenzie worries a lot. She worries about finances, friendships, and the safety of her kids. Sometimes she worries so much that her stomach hurts, she can't sleep, and her face breaks out.

"Stop worrying so much," Greg insists. "You're making yourself sick. Besides, it's stupid. What has all your worrying ever got you?"

McKenzie knows he's right, but she can't seem to stop herself. *What's wrong with me? Why do I do this to myself?* Soon she worries that she's worrying too much. "I can't stop myself," she tries to explain. "Besides, if I don't worry about things, who will? You act like nothing bothers you. At least I have a heart."

"Well, I'd rather be tough," Greg begins to shout, "than fall apart whenever things don't go just right."

McKenzie rushes out of the room, slamming the door behind her so hard that the house rattles.

Greg shakes his head. "Here we go again."

Life can be tough. Challenging things happen. And men and women often deal with the hard times differently.

Women can be like sponges. When stress rains down, they soak it up. It sinks into their pores and saturates them. Stress can totally consume them, displacing everything else. What's more, women have a hard time squeezing themselves out. They tend to hold on to stress, even when they'd rather let it go.

Women have several mental strategies when confronted with stress, and each of them increases a woman's basic sponginess.

1. Women tend to **overanalyze** the situation—contemplating, evaluating, worrying about every detail. This amplifies the negatives and increases the stress.

2. Women quickly **admit** to themselves every fear, anxiety, and worry, thus creating a hypervigilance to any potential danger and making them even more attuned to the details.

3. Women tend to **verbalize** their concerns. This can reinforce the reality and increase the magnitude of whatever difficulties are currently weighing them down.

4. Women **socialize** what they think and feel, often with other women, who add their agreement. (This is one way women affirm each other.) This legitimizes the validity of their concerns, raising their level of alarm.

5. Women **connect** their current worrisome situations with past situations they've experienced, heard about, or even read about. This universalizes their concerns, making them feel more real and more urgent.

Studies show that women are generally more stressed than men. When I ask women about this, they tell me that their minds attach to a concern, and they turn it over and over in their thoughts, considering what went wrong, what *might* go wrong, or what *they* did wrong. In other words, women think too much.

Men? Men are like turtles. When stress rains down on them, it usually rolls right off their backs. There are a lot of reasons for this:

1. Men tend to **deny** whenever they aren't sure what to do. They don't like to admit their uncertainty or helplessness.

2. Men are more likely to **ignore** details, especially negative or problematic details. This diminishes the intensity of their stress.

3. Men **suppress** "unmanly" emotions like fear, anxiety, and worry. If men don't acknowledge them, they must not exist.

4. Men **compartmentalize** their anxiety and pack it away where they don't have to think about it. They are concerned that if they think too much about a problem, they will start worrying. Compartmentalize…no worries.

5. Men like to **strategize** how to fix the situation that created the stress, thus making them more proactive, more positive, and more powerful in conquering stress.

But not all turtles are the same. Some have harder shells, which keep out all forms of stress. Some have softer shells, which selectively block certain stressors, letting others in.

Though men are generally more stress resistant, they are also more stressed than they admit. Admission of stress or worry seems like weakness to them, so they often deny the reality of stress to themselves and to others. They're not being purposefully dishonest; they just don't see what they don't *want* to see. My father insisted that stress didn't affect him, but all who knew him well sensed his tension.

Men often don't notice the symptoms of stress because they don't attend to the details until those details become so big that they hit them over the head. That's why men minimize stress symptoms like teeth grinding, sighing, low-grade headaches, compulsive oral fixations (eating, drinking, smoking, chewing), sleep troubles, irritability, and generally not feeling well. If they do notice these things, men are likely to externalize them, saying, "It's a bad day" or "The kids are driving me crazy." Men project fault rather than recognize personal impact.

Sometimes women frankly envy the turtleness of men. They resent at least some of their own spongelike qualities. They wish they weren't as anxious as they sometimes get. At times they wish they had a protective shell, even though they frequently think of their husbands as hardhearted, naive, insensitive, unconcerned, or careless.

One of the tendencies turtles and sponges have is overcompensation. If a husband is a strong turtle who doesn't notice problems or doesn't do anything about them, his wife becomes a strong sponge. She feels like she has to pay *more* attention and be *more* concerned to make up for his inattention and lack of concern. He then sees how worried and stressed she is, so he becomes even more turtlelike in order to show her there's nothing to worry about.

This strategy doesn't work. Each partner's overcompensation only reinforces the other's, rather than helping them both to moderate. She sees Mr. Teflon's imperviousness as rejection or abandonment, and he sees Mrs. Gluetrap's obsessiveness as hysterical overemotionality.

Sadly, all these reactions are the result of a pair of simple facts: he's a turtle; she's a sponge.

A friend of mine just read this chapter and started laughing.

"What's so funny?" I asked.

"Well," he said, trying to be diplomatic, "I think what you're trying to say is that men are hardheaded and women are soft-hearted."

"Not…exactly," I said. "But close enough."

TRANSLATION GUIDE

Men: Her "I won't let go of this problem" really means "I wish I could let go, but it's hard."

Women: His "I don't care about your problem" really means "I've got enough stress, and I can't add that one to the pile right now."

1. In what ways are each of you a sponge or a turtle?
2. Which of the five qualities of sponges (page 34) and the five qualities of turtles (page 35) fit your relationship?
3. How can each of you be more sensitive to the other's basic sponginess or turtleness?

EIGHT

Why the Knight Wears Armor

W hy didn't you just kill me?"

Angie was caught completely off guard by Rod's anger. "What are you talking about?" she asked. "Why are you so upset?"

"You just challenged me in front of my friends," Rod said, his face red, his bunched knuckles white. "You made me look weak and stupid. How could you do that to me?"

She rolled her eyes. "I just corrected your facts. You had the details all wrong."

"I don't give a rip about the details. You totally humiliated me in public. I can never face those people again."

"Don't be silly—"

"You ever do that again…," Rod interrupted, "you *ever* do that again, and it's over."

Most men would rather die than be humiliated publicly. Few women understand how strongly men feel about this. Very early in life, men learn a certain code of conduct. Rarely do men talk openly about this code, but then rarely do men talk openly about anything deeply personal. Yet it's there, built into his bones and reinforced by culture in hundreds of subtle and not-so-subtle ways. Men live by this code, even if they can't put it into words, even when they realize it's irrational, unrealistic, and unhealthy.

The Code goes something like this:

1. Men don't fail.
2. Men are always strong.
3. Men don't expose their weaknesses.
4. Men must be in control.
5. Men don't cry.
6. Men take care of their own problems.
7. Men don't ask for help.
8. Men must be right.
9. Men protect themselves at all costs.
10. Men don't depend on anybody.

Even though most men would adamantly deny it, they hurt just as much as women. In fact, men frequently take loss, rejection, and failure harder than women. Yet men are more likely to cover up their wounds and hold their hurt in, while women find it easier to face their wounds and let their hurt out. Because of this, men tend to experience their hurt longer, and their wounds do not heal as completely.

Rod tries to avoid his wounds through work and distractions. He doesn't feel as comfortable talking about his pain because he sees it as a sign of failure or incompetence—a minimization of his manhood. Angie views wounds as an expected part of her life experience. She's willing to admit hurts, mistakes, and weaknesses and even looks forward to talking about them as a necessary part of healing. But Rod honestly believes that making his private struggles public will only intensify his pain.

This is why most men resist any form of counseling. When a couple comes to my office for the first time, the husband is usually reluctant. When I ask him why he's here, he usually says something like:

- "She made the appointment."
- "I don't know."
- "Because she insisted."
- "She thinks it's important."
- "I'd be in big trouble if I didn't."
- "She's got some things she needs to talk about."

When I ask her why she's here, she usually gives me a carefully thought-out, detailed list of the major and minor difficulties in the marriage. She tells me when each problem began, how it affects her emotionally, and what the two of them have done to try to resolve it.

As she speaks, he looks highly uncomfortable. He might dispute the details, but he usually agrees on the major issues. When she's finished, I turn to her and say, "You are very lucky. This guy must love you a great deal to move totally out of his comfort zone and come to this appointment with you. I hope you realize how difficult this is for him."

Then I turn to him and say, "You've got a lot of guts. I'm glad you're here to fight for your marriage. I'm not here to harass you for mistakes you both might have made. I'm here to coach you so you can play the game better. Every good athlete needs a coach to help him be his very best."

By this time the husband is usually pretty relaxed and ready to talk. He's willing to risk because I've acknowledged his courage and I'm speaking his language.

Men tend to not talk about their hurts or problems unless things have gotten so out of control that there seems to be no other option. They see speaking openly about their difficulties as risking embarrassment and loss of respect. Therefore they keep things private and refuse to "air their dirty laundry." They don't go to counselors, physicians, or pastors to deal with personal issues unless they're in dire straits. Women say, "Let's catch the problem early and deal with it before it gets too big." Men tend to say, "This isn't that big of an issue. Let's just wait and see if it works itself out."

Sharing their hurts and struggles is one of the ways women connect with one another and build bonds of friendship. It's an opportunity to affirm, encourage, and identify with one another. Other women usually come alongside to empathize and build up the suffering one. So she comes to see sharing as strongly positive. Women won't go public with just anyone, but they do have a much wider range of trusted individuals than most men. Women will also trust more readily and give unproven confidantes the benefit of the doubt.

Women assume the best, and if someone betrays them, they will exclude that person from their share list. Men tend to assume the worst, and they keep their share list to just a handful of people, if anyone. They see everyone as a potential betrayer who is ready to use personal information to undermine, belittle, or destroy them. They see life as a competition; showing any weakness might give their opponents an unfair advantage. Men believe the only way to trust people is to watch them, study them, test them, listen to them, test them again...and then maybe trust them. But probably not.

Men protect their hearts. Rather than exposing their hurts and failures, they get angry, controlling, or demanding. It's when men feel vulnerable that they often become the most defensive. They frequently overcompensate with a hypermasculinity that pushes people away. Or they may withdraw into work, hobbies, projects, sports, television, addictions, or almost anything that creates distance from potential exposure.

Years ago I saw a painting that perfectly portrayed this male-female dichotomy. I wanted to buy it, but Tami insisted it was totally inappropriate for home or office. As usual, she was right.

But still, it was an intriguing picture. It portrayed a knight, strong and mighty, every portion of his head and body completely covered with shining armor. He was an untouchable warrior, ready for battle. In his outstretched arms he carried a fair maiden, completely naked and exposed—not a stitch of clothing. The contrast was shocking.

The name of the painting, obviously focusing on the woman, was *Vulnerability*.

From the other side of the gender dialogue, it just as easily could have been titled *Invulnerability*.

TRANSLATION GUIDE

Women: His resistance to opening up really means "I'm terrified of the risks of vulnerability."

Men: Her willingness to go public with her struggles means "I need to connect with people, especially with you."

1. Which of the ten components of The Code (page 39) does he believe in?
2. Men, what seems to be at stake when you risk opening up?
3. In what ways is she more open and public with her inner hurts and struggles?

NINE

More Blessed to Receive...

G uys, let me give you a quick lesson on how to make your wife feel...

- disregarded
- rejected
- lonely
- unloved
- unimportant
- insecure
- distant
- angry
- depressed

The secret? Don't listen to her.

Most women are verbal, so they frequently use words to connect with their husbands. When she shares her joys, frustrations, experiences, and observations, she feels close to you. Words are a warm blanket she wishes you both could snuggle into. Words are her safety line to you.

If a man doesn't listen, his wife often feels as if she's been slapped in the face or worse. One of the top reasons women give for considering divorce is "He doesn't listen to me or take me seriously."

Over and over again I hear from hurt and frustrated women who feel they have lost their voice. Not because they aren't speaking, but because their husbands aren't listening. For a woman to lose her voice is like a man losing his identity. Yes, a woman is obviously more than her words, but it's through her voice that she expresses her heart and soul and projects her vulnerable *self* out into the real world.

In general, women are better listeners than men. That doesn't mean that men think listening is unimportant. It's just that men and women tend to listen in different ways. Most men are naturally selective listeners; they have to work hard at *total listening*—one of the most affirming and loving gifts they can give their wives. Women are usually total listeners. They need to learn to speak in ways that can profoundly help their husbands hear them better. If both partners work on it, their relationship will improve.

Sometimes the hardest part of helping a man to listen is getting his attention. Glen, for example, honestly believes he can listen to Susan while he's doing something else, like watching TV, reading the newspaper, paying the bills, working on a home project, or almost anything. The problem is that Glen and Susan have different definitions for listening. Glen, like most men, views listening as hearing the important words and catching the general gist of what is being said. However, Susan represents women in viewing listening as hearing every word. (After all, aren't they all important?) To her, listening is also hearing *between the lines* to catch emotions, needs, expectations, and real meaning. Glen thinks he's doing great if he absorbs every fifth word and then fills in the spaces with what makes sense to him (which might end up bearing no resemblance to what Susan is trying to communicate).

Another difficulty is that men tend to have shorter attention spans when it comes to listening to their wives. Glen can usually give his total focus for the first few minutes—sometimes even as long as five minutes.

But after that he's gone. Susan needs to understand that under a barrage of too many words, men frequently...

- tune out or daydream.
- get overwhelmed.
- feel stressed.
- lose interest.
- forget where the conversation began.
- become lost in the details.
- listen partially.
- become distracted by something else on their minds.

Glen doesn't do any of these things to purposefully annoy Susan. It's just the way men are. I'm not saying this is right; I'm just saying it's reality. Susan can rant and rave about it, but that won't change Glen's basic maleness. And her ranting might exasperate him into becoming stubborn.

A compromise that frequently works is for Susan to front-load the first two minutes of the conversation with the most important information. Glen, for his part, promises to give full attention during those two minutes and to repeat back the main point when she's finished. This gives him no valid reason for not listening.

It also keeps his mind from wandering with questions like *When will this ever end? What is the point she's getting to?* and *How do I fix this?* I realize that these questions are probably offensive to many women; that's the reason smart husbands don't say them out loud. Still, though these thoughts are common to most men, these same men fully love and adore their wives. It's just that listening comes hard to them.

Another common difficulty is that men can read only one level of communication at a time. Most women communicate on a number of different levels simultaneously—using words, emotions, tone of voice, facial expressions, and body language, to name just a few. When Glen focuses on words, he will probably miss the emotional nuances behind them. For example, if he asks whether anything is wrong, and Susan says, "No, not really," she assumes he can clearly hear in her voice that something is definitely wrong. But he takes her at her word and drops the subject, satisfied.

Or if he focused on her tone of voice or the intensity of her emotions, he might be too distracted to catch her words. Sometimes when Glen simply sees the expression on his wife's face or the way she is standing, he finds it hard to listen to what she is saying. He doesn't mean to ignore the total message; he's just wired to listen to one level at a time.

None of these male realities let men off the hook, though. Men need to do all they can to be fully present when their wives are speaking—looking and listening with all their being. Just as men need their wives to be sexually attentive, so women need their husbands to be verbally attentive. It's not easy to give 100 percent focus, but it can be done.

Here are a few dos and don'ts for listening to anyone:

1. Look at the speaker.
2. Clear your mind of distractions.
3. Ask yourself, "What is she (or he) trying to say?"
4. Seek clarification if you don't understand.
5. Repeat back what you heard.
6. Thank the person for sharing with you.
7. Avoid shutting down when uncomfortable.
8. Stay attentive even when you don't like what you hear.
9. Don't get defensive or overreact.
10. Be careful not to interrupt.

It's through listening that a couple comes to better understand each other. The wisest man in the world, King Solomon, said it this way: "The way of a fool seems right to him, but a wise man listens to advice"

(Proverbs 12:15). Though I have written much of this toward men, it applies to both sexes. Listening opens the door to communication, and communication truly does lead to closeness. It's hard work, but well worth it.

If either partner refuses to listen, your marriage is headed for rough waters. But if both of you listen, you'll create a friendship that's an oasis in a dry and lonely desert.

TRANSLATION GUIDE

Men: To her, listening means "I want you to hear *everything* I say and also the emotions I'm implying."

Women: His seeming inattention really means "My ability to listen is limited, so please help me get the most important information."

1. When is it hardest for you to listen to your spouse?
2. How would each of you rate your listening to the other (on a scale of 1 = "terrible" to 10 = "fantastic")? Why?
3. Which of the suggestions on page 46 do you need to implement to improve your listening skills?

TEN

Where Many Men Have Gone Before

S *pace.* By no means the final frontier. For men, that is. For millenniums, men have found space to be a source of comfort and revitalization.

Sometimes I need space. And when I do, I like to wander into my backyard, where life is peaceful and quiet. It's usually early evening, when the sun is low and the shadows long. I casually stroll across the creek and walk around randomly, looking at the landscape, pulling a few weeds, trimming some dead branches off the trees. I enjoy this time alone. It feels refreshing to escape the craziness of the everyday world. I walk alongside the creek and find a shady place to sit on its bank. *This would be a great place to build a second bridge—something simple.* I plan out how to build it, what it would look like, what supplies I would need. It's a nice dream. *Maybe I'll get Dusty or Dylan to help me. We can do it next weekend.* After some fifteen or twenty minutes I return to the house, feeling so much better. I give Tami a kiss. I'm ready to jump back into family life.

I just needed some space.

Why? Maybe I was tired after a long day's work. Maybe I needed some time to think. Maybe my stress was high. Maybe I was at a loss for the solution to a problem.

Maybe I didn't know why I needed space; I just felt the longing for time alone.

Every man periodically needs this sort of escape. It helps him think, relax, regroup, reenergize, catch his breath. Space nurtures a man's soul. In earlier times, men would take to the open sea, explore new lands, ride the range, go hunting. There is still a place in every man's heart that likes to get away. From among the thousand ways to do this, he might…

- turn on the TV.
- get lost on the Internet.
- go fishing.
- play golf.
- hike or jog.
- work out.
- dive into a hobby or project.
- stay at work later.

In such ways a man claims his space, his time alone. Yet from a woman's perspective a healthy relationship should be close. And the closer, the better. Too much space feels dangerous and lonely. When her husband is claiming his space, she tends to think, and maybe ask, "Why don't you do anything with me?" or "Don't you like spending time with me?" This is an attempt to get him to draw closer and reassure her. Unfortunately, if she comes across too hostile or clingy, it often makes him feel controlled or smothered, causing him to seek even more space.

Tami doesn't always understand why I need my quiet retreat into the woods of my backyard. But it's crucial to my sanity.

Both space and closeness are legitimate needs. And every relationship requires a balance of both. With too much space a relationship can get disconnected, and the marriage starts looking like two roommates rather than a couple. Yet with too much closeness a relationship gets so enmeshed that each partner loses his and her individual identity. Khalil

Gibran wrote, "Let there be spaces in your togetherness." Along with times of closeness, healthy couples also create times of distance where they encourage each other's personal pursuits and development.

A man usually needs space during times of conflict. When men feel frustrated, overwhelmed, blamed, overpowered, disrespected, or humiliated, they tend to react with two defenses. They either attack or withdraw, or sometimes attack and then withdraw. (I call this hit-and-run.) When they withdraw, it's often because they realize that an attack—emotional, verbal, or physical—doesn't accomplish much positive. So withdrawing seems the safest and most rational option.

But this strikes fear to the woman's heart. She finds comfort in closeness, so when a husband withdraws, a wife tends to pursue. She wants to make sure everything is okay. But the more she approaches, the more he avoids. Not because he doesn't love his wife, but because he feels overwhelmed. He's not rejecting her; he desperately wants space to calm himself down and figure things out.

His wife should let him go, but this is where a good husband can give his wife the dose of reassurance she needs while explaining what he needs most in the moment. Simply tell her in a calm tone of voice these five things:

1. "I need space."
2. "This is where I'm going."
3. "This is when I'll return."
4. "This is when we can continue this conversation."
5. "We can work this out."

Now his wife can have the confidence that she is not being rejected or ignored.

Another reason a man might need some space is because he feels misunderstood, shamed, or vulnerable—especially if he feels he has failed at providing, protecting, parenting, or marriage. This discomfort drives a man into silence and isolation so he can work it through. Without this time alone, he can easily and quickly feel backed into a corner, where he is likely to lash out with unthought-out words he will later regret.

Space energizes men. A few minutes strolling through my backyard can change my whole attitude. It can make men more relaxed, less reactive, and generally more positive to be with. So here are some constructive ways a wife can give her husband space:

1. Encourage him to spend time with his friends.
2. Ask fewer questions.
3. Nurture peace in the home.
4. Allow silence.
5. Make sure he has his own space at home.
6. Promote his hobbies.
7. Thank him for what he does.
8. Watch television together.
9. Give him time alone.
10. Remember that you don't have to do everything together.

For women, safety comes from closeness and connection. For men, safety comes from space and distance. Yet when men are struggling, they need closeness more than they realize. The problem isn't that they despise closeness; they just don't trust it. They must feel safe in order to willingly become vulnerable.

Giving space shows respect and honor to a man. Giving closeness shows love and affirmation to a woman. These are both important; neither strategy is wrong. So while a woman must allow a man some space, the man must remember to come back and meet his wife's needs. Talk, listen, hold hands, go on a date, write a note, plan a trip, pray with her. Help her dissolve the feelings of worthlessness that can build when she's left alone for too long. Let her feel loved and cared for. Tami lets me have my space periodically, and I plan times of closeness periodically. We both accept the differences; because of that we love each other even more.

I'm back to walking through my yard once again. The daylilies are blooming, and the blackberries are ripe. I strolled across my new bridge just a bit ago, jumping up and down on it a few times to make sure it's solid. Then I congratulated myself on how good it looks.

I gaze back at our home and think about how blessed I am. Then I wander through the trees, thinking about Tami and the kids. *What would be fun for us all to do tonight?* All sorts of ideas fill my head as I start to walk toward the house with a sense of excitement. My time alone has been great, and now I'm ready for some togetherness.

Tami asks what I've been up to. (She always asks.) I smile and say, "Nothing. I just needed some space." Then I move my hands from behind my back to show her what I brought for her—a bouquet of daylilies and a handful of blackberries.

She kisses my cheek and says, "Next time let's walk together."

I return her kiss and say, "Maybe."

TRANSLATION GUIDE

Women: His "I need space" means "I love you, but I can't unwind and work out my stress unless I have time alone."

Men: Her "I need closeness" means "It's hard for me to feel secure and relaxed unless I have positive time with you."

1. In what ways does he seek space? When does he need this most?

2. In what ways does she seek closeness? When does she need this most?

3. Women, which ideas from page 51 are you willing to use to provide what your husband needs?

ELEVEN

To Be or Not to Be

Tami and I just had a fight.

It came out of nowhere. But it seems strangely familiar because I think we've had this fight many times before. Most couples don't have incredibly original fights; they just visit the same old ground over and over again. Tami and I are no different. In fact, I even have a name for this fight. It's our "vacation fight."

We started this fight on our honeymoon in romantic Hawaii. We were lying by the pool in Maui, relaxing and having a great time, when I started putting together an exciting agenda of all the fascinating places we could explore on the island. "Tami, just look at everything we can do," I said with great enthusiasm. "This afternoon we can explore this side of the island and then visit Lahaina. Tomorrow we can go to the top of the volcano for sunrise and hike around the mountain. The day after that let's take the long, winding road to Hana and see the sights. I hear it's beautiful."

Tami looked at me in disbelief. "Why can't we just relax by the pool and enjoy our time together? Why do we have to do anything?"

My mind reeled in an attempt to understand this concept. How could we *not* do anything? I'd never been to Hawaii. There were places to explore, mountains to conquer, adventures to pursue, oceans to swim, sights to see, paths to hike. And I wanted to share all those experiences with my fantastic bride, but all she wanted to do was relax by my side and visit. In my frustration I said something like, "We have the rest of our lives to visit, but we might never be back to Hawaii again."

Seeing my determination and wanting to avoid a conflict, she graciously did it my way. Most of our honeymoon was a wild—and somewhat exhausting—adventure. In return, I very sensitively set aside one day to relax around the pool and do nothing.

Men like to do. We like to be active and physical. We are explorers and adventurers. We want to hunt and conquer and achieve. We like to do new things, challenging things, different things, "manly" things.

Women like to be. This doesn't mean they don't do a lot and periodically enjoy engaging in exciting or physical activities. But women are more comfortable simply existing in the moment without having to conquer or explore anything. To them a good conversation or a pleasant book can be just as satisfying as, and sometimes more so than, a great adventure. A quiet walk on the beach, casually picking up shells and talking about the kids, can be the best part of the journey. They can simply sit back and soak in the beauty of God's creation with no agenda.

Men have to have an agenda for everything. Even if all they want to do is relax, they feel they have to hide it behind an activity, such as fishing or golf or a business lunch.

Tami says that women must take every chance they get to relax because they don't come by many opportunities. Most women have so much to do—taking care of their husbands, children, homes, jobs, and everything else they squeeze into their schedules. They are constantly multitasking. Women tend to pace themselves. They are long-distance runners. When there is a space in their schedules, they take advantage of it for rest.

Men are sprinters. They give the race everything they've got until they're exhausted. Then they stop for a short moment, catch their breath, and do it all again. Because of this frantic style, men might accomplish more, but they...

- burn themselves out.
- frequently don't spend enough time with their families.
- sabotage their marriages.
- don't develop deep friendships.
- feel frustrated and dissatisfied with themselves.
- die younger.

Men pay a high price for their masculinity. There is much men can learn from women, and one of the most important lessons is how to just be.

Every healthy relationship needs a balance of doing and being. It is in *doing* that a couple serve each other, raise children, care for a home, and reach out to others. But it is in *being* that a couple listen to each other, lean on each other, and encourage each other. It is also through being that one hears God's voice and surrenders to His ways. It is through being that one's faith grows. As one *does*, he may be trusting in his own abilities and actions. A time comes when he must *stop* the doing and trust in God. Our actions frequently distract us from the spiritual dimension and from an eternal perspective.

Some women would do well to indulge their husbands in order to center some of their companionship around activities that he—and preferably she too—enjoys.

And most men need to do less and be more. I know this is true, but it's hard to stop doing. It's hard to not push forward. It just goes against the grain for most guys.

So here I am at a swimming pool in Puerto Vallarta, after twenty-three years of marriage, contriving an action-packed agenda for our vacation. I yearn to kayak the canal, snorkel in the ocean, and explore the jungles. I see adventure around every corner and a hundred new challenges to conquer. Let's go!

In my excitement I gush, "Tonight we can do this, and tomorrow we can do that, and the day after we can do something else. Just think of all the incredible things we can do!"

Tami looks at me in disbelief. *(Déjà vu!)* "Why can't we just relax by the pool and enjoy our time together? Why do you always have to be on the go? Why do we have to do anything?"

I'm ticked. I just want to have some fun, and my wife won't join me. I sit back and pout. A slight breeze rustles through the palm trees as the sun glistens on the cool surface of a gorgeous swimming pool. Birds chatter and then take wing across the brilliant blue skies. I stare at the rugged mountains in the distance and the brilliantly colored bougainvillea a few feet away. God sure knows how to create beauty.

The longer I sit, the more I relax. It feels good. My frustration fades. My soul grows calm. Soon all my adventurous plans seem less important. I can do them another day. If the opportunity arises.

The sun soaks into my heart, and contentment fills me. Maybe I need to slow down and just be. Maybe Tami is right.

I smile. God is so good.

A few minutes later I pick up a pad of paper and start writing this chapter. After all, I've got to have *something* to do.

TRANSLATION GUIDE

Men: Her desire to quietly *be* means "I really need a break, and so do you, and so do *we*."

Women: His desire to actively *do* means "I derive energy and self-worth from accomplishment and adventure."

1. What does he do to make her feel guilty for just being? What does she say to herself to make *herself* feel guilty?
2. What does he do to keep himself busy? What activity would be fun to do together?
3. How can you together balance the doing and being in your relationship?

TWELVE

Erotic Divergence

Sex can be great. But it can also be one of the most confusing and even hurtful aspects of a relationship. Hundreds of couples have asked me this simple question: how can something so good create so much frustration? The answer is just as simple: men and women approach sexuality from completely different points of view.

Observe Bobby. He'd had a rough day. Nothing seemed to go right. It all started with a fight with his wife, Aubrey, over a stupid misunderstanding. He ended up calling her a control freak and a few other words that are not printable. They parted angrily, and his day went downhill from there. Work was a string of frustrations, his truck broke down, his kids were whiny, and he discovered he'd overdrawn his checking account. That evening Bobby was in a terribly foul mood as he moped about the house, slamming doors and yelling at the cat.

Finally the couple crawled into bed, and Aubrey prayed that tomorrow he'd be happier. Suddenly a hand slipped onto her waist. *Oh no, not tonight!* She tried to pretend she was asleep.

"You sure look great tonight," he whispered in her ear.

Just leave me alone! she kept repeating in her head.

"I sure like snuggling with you," he said as he ran his hand up and down her thigh.

After a day like today, why in the world would I want to snuggle with a jerk like you?

"You have amazing legs."

She rolled over on her side with her back to him.

"It's been almost a week," he said as he pressed his body close to her.

And I'm supposed to be in the mood after the way you've treated me today? She continued to ignore him.

"You're such a great wife," he said as he kissed the back of her neck.

That's far from what you called me this morning. Why can't you just leave me alone? She tightened her jaw, determined that she wouldn't cry.

"Does this feel good?" He moved his hand to her breast.

"Could you just leave me alone!" she shouted as she pushed his hand away. "All I want to do is sleep."

He quietly retreated, honestly bewildered. *What's wrong with her? Can't a husband even show his wife how much he loves her without getting his head bitten off?*

Not only were these two on different pages—they were in different books…written in different languages…in different universes!

Men view sex as equal to love. We know this isn't always true, but that's how it feels. If the sexual relationship is good, everything is good. Therefore men often see sex as a cure-all for every sort of relationship difficulty.

Women view sex and love as totally separate topics. Sex can be wonderful, but it doesn't solve other problems; talking does.

Men and women both desire closeness and intimacy, but their

methods of gaining these are different. Men use sex. Women use communication. So women ask their husbands, "Is sex all you ever think about?" and men ask their wives, "Why is it you always want to talk?" The reality is that both have valuable pieces of the puzzle. If they would combine their perspectives, they would discover that closeness and intimacy require both. Let's deal with the sexual half of the picture in this chapter.

Most women love to communicate. Except about sex. Guys will joke about sex, but they too avoid talking seriously about it. That's why one of the greatest areas of misunderstanding in marriages stays so misunderstood.

"But it's awkward."

"It's embarrassing."

"He'll get aroused."

"She'll feel pressured."

"It will lead to a fight."

"It just seems weird to talk about it."

These are a few of the excuses I've heard. But in spite of the difficulty, talking about sexuality is a prerequisite for any improvement. Communication is the only way to overcome the large gap between men and women. In fact, there are many sexual gaps. If a couple can understand these differences, they can learn how to bridge them. So let's explore a few.

The Anticipation Gap. Sex is on men's minds a lot—typically just a thought away. Sexual thoughts come quickly and often spontaneously. Most women rarely think about sex without some reminder. This is hard for most men to believe, just as it's hard for women to believe that men think so much about it. Men are sexual optimists, hoping their wives might be open to sexual encounters at any time, anywhere, at a moment's notice. Women are more pragmatic. A certain number of specific factors have to fall perfectly into place for them to feel arousal. Women have a hard time being sexually intimate unless they are "in the mood." Men are *always* in the mood. They also believe they can lead their wives there, if only given a chance. And in fact, many wives are surprised to discover that a patient, loving husband can accomplish this feat when she honestly thought it was impossible.

The Testosterone Gap. Testosterone is one of the hormones that makes a man a man. Men have high levels of testosterone, and women have low levels. Sexual desire in men is a hormone-driven urge, determined largely by the level of testosterone in his body. Men don't have to choose to be aroused; sometimes it just happens, like when they wake up aroused straight out of a good night's sleep. This doesn't mean that men can't or shouldn't work regularly on controlling their arousal. Men are much more than their hormones. Testosterone explains a man's high sexual drive, but it's never an excuse for rude, demanding, or abusive sexual attitudes.

The Visual Gap. Men are very visually oriented, and when they see sexual stimuli, they are almost immediately aroused. Men find their attention almost irresistibly drawn to attractive women, billboards, magazines, and TV commercials. And they're surrounded by these stimuli almost everywhere they go. Men like to look. The problem is *where* they look. It's wonderful for a man to look at his own wife. But it's dangerous, unhealthy, and downright wrong to look with sexual interest at someone to whom he is not married. Interestingly enough, as a man's testosterone level goes down, so does the power of visual stimuli. And sexual release reduces testosterone levels. So regular sexual intimacy can reduce the danger that a man will give in to visual temptations.

The Emotional Gap. Most men find that, more than almost anything else, a sexual connection opens their hearts to emotional closeness. Yet most women need an emotional connection before they are fully interested in opening their bodies to sexual intimacy. To most men, physical oneness equals emotional oneness. This seems absurd to most women, who think, *I want to know he wants me for who I am, not just my body.* Women yearn to be loved, not just sexually desired. Therefore romance, tenderness, and communication say to a woman that she is valued and treasured. If her husband takes the time and effort to meet her emotional needs, then she feels loved and is usually very open to meet his sexual needs (and to enjoy it fully in the process).

The Security Gap. Women feel a need for love and security, which then leads to a desire for sex. Men see sex as the ultimate proof of love and security. Therefore when men feel insecure or disconnected in their relationships, they desire sex. Yet when women feel insecure or disconnected in their relationships, sex is the last thing on their minds. They crave the comfort and security of resolution; only then can they relax and fully enjoy the pleasures of sex. The more they relax, the faster they will be aroused and the more satisfying that arousal will be. For women, relaxation can lead to sex, while for most men, sex leads to relaxation. Sexuality can distract a man from almost any frustration or difficulty, reducing his physical and emotional stress.

If sex is one of the things getting lost in translation, a couple who bridges these gaps will likely find that the problems aren't as difficult as they thought. Most problems involving sexuality are very fixable, but the solutions start with trying to understand the differences and openly talking about them. Here is hope: every couple can have a better, more fulfilling physical relationship—and with it a closeness that makes the marriage deeper and stronger.

And a lot more fun.

TRANSLATION GUIDE

Women: His "sex obsession" really means "I need sex in order to feel close to you."

Men: Her "sex resistance" really means "How can we have sex when we're not close yet?"

1. What keeps the two of you from talking about your sexual differences and frustrations?
2. Which of the five gaps are most apparent in your relationship?
3. What does each of you appreciate the most about your sexual relationship?

THIRTEEN

Handle with Care

Kristen declines Joe's advances simply because her hormone cycle is in the "low interest" phase.

Sarah, a mother of three preschoolers, barely drags herself to bed most nights. No wonder sex is the last thing on her mind.

Emily is so ticked off at her husband that if he touches her, she will… Well, he'd just better not touch her.

Andrea doesn't feel very sexy.

Sandy can't relax.

Tia's brain is racing: *What should I fix for dinner tomorrow? Is Colleen mad at me? When am I going to get that paperwork finished?*

Other items that can block or significantly reduce a woman's desire include:

- distractions
- aches or pains
- negative sexual history
- sexual insecurity
- medications
- personal hygiene

To a woman, many of these obstacles feel as if they are out of her control. Men believe these same barriers can be easily overcome if a woman really wants to.

Part of this radical difference comes from the astounding complexity of women in this area. Very few things block a man's sexual desire. Yet men have been deceived by media—movies, television, books, magazines, and music—into thinking that women have a much higher sex drive than they actually do. Most women do enjoy their sexual relationship with their husbands. But they enjoy it best when it is orchestrated, while men tend to be fairly impulsive and impromptu.

Women need to feel positive about their men to have the most fulfilling sexual experiences. They need loving, caring, connecting contexts. They need to be romantically pursued outside the bedroom. Hundreds of women have asked me, "Why is it the only time my husband is nice to me when he wants sex?" or "Why is it the only time he really listens to me is in the bedroom?" Men need to learn how to be more romantic 24/7. They need to perfect the art of affirming, encouraging, and complimenting their wives; of quality conversation and total listening; of helping with the everyday household chores without being asked; of watching what movies and television shows she wants; of giving gifts (they don't have to be expensive) and nonsexual touch (that doesn't have to lead anywhere). As men show sensitivity and love in a few simple ways, they might be surprised at how quickly their wives' hearts open to something more intimate.

Another difference has a strong physiological base: women take more time to reach arousal and climax than men—as much as ten times as long. So even when a woman is interested in sex, she needs to prepare herself emotionally and allow herself to relax before she can even begin a healthy sexual connection. Since women tend to be more stress-sensitive than men, and since stress is one of women's main blocks to desire, women need to intentionally de-stress themselves. A calm bath, a gentle back massage, a romantic movie, or a positive conversation can help relax her and can set the stage for a powerful sexual connection.

However, in this hectic, fast-paced world, both men and women easily become impatient. Men are usually aroused very quickly, so they have a hard time slowing down and getting in sync with their wives. Thus women try to speed themselves up, which increases their stress and delays their arousal even further. If the man can slow down, enjoy the moment, and gently focus on pleasing her, the results will turn out much more positively for both partners. She will sense his love and sensitivity, which will bring her to arousal more quickly. And if he can distract himself until she reaches climax, then he can immediately allow himself to go. In this way a couple's sexuality becomes mutually arousing and satisfying. It also becomes a true statement of love.

Now, men are more fragile than they let on, and they require a different kind of sensitivity from their wives. Sex is incredibly emotionally fulfilling to most men. Sex shows a man that his wife...

- wants him.
- needs him.
- loves him.
- appreciates him.
- accepts him.
- makes him a priority.

Sex energizes a man. It makes him feel better about himself, while it also enhances his appreciation of and commitment to his wife. Yet what truly brings him sexual fulfillment—and a sense of healthy self-worth—is pleasing his wife sexually. Even though men frequently have a stronger sexual drive, most men do not want to be sexually insensitive. They care deeply about their wives' feelings. That's why the following can undermine a man's masculinity faster than anything else:

- A wife who doesn't seem to even think about sex (except how to avoid it)
- A wife who consistently rejects or ignores her husband sexually
- A wife whose attitude is: "Okay, I'm here. Let's get this over with as quickly as possible."

These deflate a man quickly and completely, leaving him feeling rejected and like a failure—in the bedroom, in the marriage, and in life.

Men are greatly affirmed by women who take the sexual relationship seriously. When women are willing to talk about it, plan for it, and do all they can to improve it, their husbands feel a closeness to their wives that can't be achieved any other way. In fact, something is seriously wrong if a man shows little or no sexual interest in his wife. This may be a sign that he has fallen out of love, has given up on his marriage, is deeply depressed, or has succumbed to a serious temptation. Women need to actively promote and nurture a healthy sexual bond.

Still, men need to carefully avoid sexual greed, just as women need to carefully avoid sexual frugality. Every couple should learn to be generous with both their sensitivity and their sexuality. These two merge into a *sensitive sexuality*, affirming and making the most of the wonderful differences between husbands and wives.

This issue came up as I spoke to Jody and Allen. I encouraged Jody to be very careful about ignoring or avoiding Allen's advances. Then I told Allen to be equally aware of Jody's level of comfort and openness.

"So I shouldn't say no unless I really need to," Jody said.

"But I shouldn't push ahead sexually," said Allen, "unless I sense she is truly open."

"You've got it," I replied with a smile.

That is balance.

That is sexual sensitivity.

That is love.

TRANSLATION GUIDE

Men: Her "disinterest" in sex really means "I honestly need your sensitivity and help to get past the distractions and blocks to my sexual interest."

Women: His interest in sex really means "I honestly need your sensitivity and availability to affirm my masculinity and self-worth."

1. What most commonly blocks or reduces her sexual desire?
2. How do the two of you define sexuality differently?
3. What are two ways you wish your spouse would show more sexual sensitivity to you?

FOURTEEN

Butterflies and Buffaloes

Y ou never take me seriously." Trudy was livid.

"That's not fair," Stu said. "I take everything you say very seriously."

"That's a bold-faced lie, and you know it! Every day for the past five years I've asked you to pick up your clothes off our bedroom floor, and do you do it? No way! You totally ignore my words and expect me to be your personal maid."

"Wait a minute." Stu knew now that he had an airtight case, and he was ready to fight for justice. "I can't believe what I just heard. You have never asked me to pick up my clothes. If you had, I would've done it. In fact, a lot of times I plan to clean things up—all on my own. But you beat me to it. I've never expected you to do it all. I thought you were just being nice, doing part of my work. But I guess I got that all wrong."

Trudy stood dumbfounded, staring at her husband with a combination of hurt and anger. She took a deep breath to calm herself down. "Don't I, every day, say something like, 'Our bedroom is a mess. There are dirty clothes everywhere'?"

"Yes, you do."

"See!" Trudy declared in triumph. "Finally you admit that you heard me ask you to pick up your clothes!"

"But you didn't ask me to pick up my clothes," Stu insisted. "You simply pointed out the condition of the room, and I agreed with you."

"Stuart, why would I point out the condition of the room unless it was to let you see what a slob you are in hopes you'll do something about it?"

"But you didn't out-and-out ask me. I had no idea that's what you were getting at."

"Do I have to spell everything out in order for you to get it?" Trudy stared in genuine disbelief.

"Yes," Stu answered a little more quietly. "Yes, I think that's exactly what you need to do. Maybe I'm slow, but until this very minute I didn't realize what you were trying to say to me. Or how important it was to you."

"I've been telling you for five years." She started to break down.

Stu took her hand. "I'm sorry. I honestly never understood. Next time could you just tell me in plain old English? Direct and to the point?"

Sound familiar? Hundreds of times I've been asked two simple questions:

- "Why doesn't he understand me?"
- "Why is she so mad at me?"

As with so many other frustrations in marriage, the answers to these two questions come down to different communication and thinking styles. The bottom line is, women are like butterflies and men are like buffaloes.

Butterflies are beautiful and subtle. They flit around; it's hard to tell exactly where they're going to land. Women dance around issues, sending out all sorts of hints and indirect signals. They think these are perfectly clear, obvious for anyone to understand. After all, their girlfriends always know what they mean, so why wouldn't their husbands?

But men are buffaloes. They notice only that which is obvious, unambiguous, crystal-clear. A woman often believes that her messages are so explicit that they can't be missed. Therefore, if her husband doesn't pick up on them, she assumes he must be selfish, insensitive, mad at her, or just uncaring. So because of his obliviousness, now she feels hurt, lonely, unloved, and angry. He can't figure out why she's so moody, so he withdraws to let her cool down. That just makes things worse.

This is another area where women are more complex than men. Women hint and beat around the bush. They hide their meaning between the lines of what they say. But men are terrible mind readers; they seldom see anything but the lines—nothing between. Men are buffaloes—what you see is what you get, and what they say is what they mean. Kathryn Morris, an actress in the television show *Cold Case*, puts it this way: "Men really mean what they're saying. You can pretty much take it at face value." Men speak black-and-white, and they're baffled when women speak gray.

Men are blunt and to the point. They want to get to the bottom line as quickly as possible. When someone asks a man a question, he provides a direct answer to the specific question that was asked. He responds with brief, honest answers—simply yes or no whenever possible. Women tend to perceive directness as rude or tactless. Tami has frequently accused me of these traits, when all I'm doing is being honest. (I can only assume she wanted an honest response; after all, she asked!)

When women are asked a question, they answer it indirectly, in accordance with the rules of appropriateness. They use some complicated relational formula that takes into account what the person is "really asking," how the person is feeling at the time, how it might impact the relationship, and who might be listening. (These issues don't even create a blip on a man's radar.) Also, women answer questions with paragraphs rather than short sentences. Even if the question only requires a yes or no answer, women tend to explain, justify, defend, or give a context for their answer. All this makes sense if one remembers that women communicate to build relationships, while men communicate to exchange data.

One of the most frustrating things for a man is when he wants to do something nice for his wife, but she won't tell him exactly what she'd like. At that point a man usually takes his wife at her word, thinking, *She must not have any preferences.* Meanwhile, the wife usually knows exactly what she wants, but she wants him to figure it out without her telling him. (Besides, she's probably told him a hundred times before.) If she tells him what she wants, it doesn't count. If the husband figures it out without her telling him, that's proof he really loves her—that he really knows her. *Two points!*

Most men hate this game, usually because they're really bad at it. Clairvoyance didn't come as standard equipment from the factory.

If wives would directly tell their husbands what they want, most husbands would gladly do it. But if women only hint, men probably won't get it. Winston Churchill once wrote, "If you have an important point to make, don't try to be subtle or clever. Use a pile driver. Hit the point once. Then come back and hit it again. Then hit it a third time—with a tremendous whack." I know this sounds like overkill to most women, but it's true. Women need to be bold and blunt—but not rude or disrespectful—to get their messages across. When a wife shares her heart with her husband in a clear and concise way, in most situations he will do everything within his power to meet her wants and needs. If, however, she becomes demanding, mean, or sarcastic—treating him like a fool—the stubborn buffalo comes out, snorting and stamping his hoofs.

Men, for their part, would do well to remember that their wives are speaking in their natural language—not purposefully trying to be vague. They should get into the habit of asking, humbly and lovingly, for clear, direct communication.

A couple hours after their earlier fight, Trudy shook her head. "How could we have missed each other's message so badly?"

"Maybe butterflies don't speak loud enough for buffaloes to hear," Stu broke in.

"Well, maybe buffaloes are hard of hearing," Trudy responded.

They both laughed.

"Why don't I just pick up my clothes off the bedroom floor?" Stu volunteered.

"I'd love it if you'd do that for me."

"No problem." Then after a moment or two Stu added, "I really am sorry it took so long to get what you wanted. I guess buffaloes can be a bit thick-skulled."

Trudy smiled and squeezed his hand. Even Stu was able to interpret such a femininely subtle gesture as her expression of agreement and appreciation.

After all, buffaloes aren't always as dense as they look.

TRANSLATION GUIDE

Women: His "I don't get it" really means "I don't get it. Please spell it out."

Men: Her indirect communication really means "I thought everyone understood my hints and inferences."

1. In what ways could men be less blunt and women be less subtle?
2. How has his bluntness created problems or misunderstandings in your relationship?
3. How has her subtleness created problems or misunderstandings?

FIFTEEN

Of Landscapes and Lilac Petals

How do I look?" Shelly made graceful, exaggerated gestures like a game show model.

"You look fabulous!" Michael said.

"Does anything about me look different?"

"No, not really," Michael said as he carefully studied her to see what he might be missing. "You always look beautiful."

"But doesn't anything look new?"

"Your top? Did you get a new top?"

"No," she snapped. "This is several months old."

A second try, more tentative. "You've…highlighted your hair."

"Well, I'm glad you noticed," she said in a sarcastic tone. "But I got it highlighted last week. Why don't you notice anything about me? Aren't I important to you anymore?"

"You are the most important thing in my life. I'd do anything for you."

"Then why didn't you notice my new earrings?" she asked, sounding a little hurt. "I got them because I thought you'd like them. I just want to look my best for you. So you'll be proud of me. So you'll love me."

"Shelly, I'm always proud of you." Michael placed his arm around her. "You are more beautiful today than when we got married. I love you. I guess I'm handicapped. I'm just not good with details."

Which brings us to another battlefield for butterflies and buffaloes: details. Butterflies love the details. They flit about from one bright-colored flower to another, enjoying the fragrance and lingering over the intricate beauty. Meanwhile buffaloes are so busy getting wherever they're going that they trample right over the flowers, not even noticing what was right under their feet.

Women love, savor, talk about, ask about, reminisce about, and generally enjoy the details. Tami and I were at a Valentine's Day banquet where each couple was encouraged to reminisce about their first date. (I'm sure a woman dreamed up the exercise.) Tami relished the chance to revisit this wonderful memory, and I was amazed at all she remembered:

- what she wore
- what I wore
- how she felt
- where we ate
- what we ordered

The list went on and on. Once she filled out the picture for me, I also remembered where we ate and that the food was good. But not a whole lot more. The details simply didn't stick in my mind.

Men focus on the big picture. To my credit, I *did* remember that it was a great date, we had a lot of fun, and Tami was a fantastic person. That's the important stuff. I could still taste the cake. But Tami, like most women, believed that it was the icing (the details) that made the cake (the big picture) meaningful.

Men cut to the chase. For most men, details get in the way. They're irrelevant distractions that keep a guy from getting to what is truly important. Men can walk into a roomful of people and never notice the details that stand out as highlights for women:

- How do the colors of the room go together?
- How recently were the floors cleaned?
- What are people wearing?
- How do they accessorize?
- Have they recently had their hair cut?
- Who looks tired, depressed, or worried?

Guys might notice these sorts of things if they're very bold and obvious. Or they might not, even though they're visual. That's one reason men aren't good at gossip; they can't get the juicy details right.

Buffaloes notice how many people are in the room, what subjects are talked about, what occupations are represented, who are the most interesting or influential individuals. Men want to know what's happening. They collect facts and exchange information. Men like to stick to nouns (Who is he?) and verbs (What does he do?), while women like adjectives (What does it look like?) and adverbs (How does she do it?). Buffaloes stampede through a room, gathering the general lay of the land. Butterflies flutter, tasting the nectar and sharing it with others.

Women think minutely. They focus on each individual tree in the forest—studying, appreciating, and sometimes even critiquing it. They notice the type of tree, along with its color, texture, and a hundred other details that make each tree unique. Men think globally. They see the forest and are unconcerned with the specific trees. For them, the details blend and blur until those details disappear into the grander picture of the whole.

It's important to realize that both the details and the big picture are crucial. The big picture provides direction and shape. The details provide beauty and life. The big picture without the details would become dull, empty, colorless. Likewise, the details without the big picture would fall into a jumble of randomness, uselessness, and irrelevance. But when put together, they create a full and beautiful portrait—much more powerful and positive than either one standing alone. Often a couple's differences are incredibly complementary, if only they would let them work together rather than fighting over which one is better.

Buffaloes and butterflies also differ with respect to the details of social etiquette. Butterflies are gentle. They interface with their environment carefully, politely, not wanting to shake things up. The Rules are written on their hearts, instinctively ready at hand. Buffaloes are bold and scruffy. They burst purposefully through their environment, frequently failing to notice that they might have offended someone. And if they do, they believe they'll be forgiven because they're buffaloes. Manners seem useless as men pursue their goals. A man can be like a bull—I mean a buffalo—in a china shop.

It's good that someone can see the big picture, or some of life's most important tasks would never be accomplished. I urge women to be patient with these sometimes ogre-like foreigners called men. Yet without the details, relationships become strained, argumentative, and potentially disconnected.

Speaking as a man, my life is far too full of details; I'm confident that some can be ignored or forgotten. But for any man who wishes to touch the heart of his wife and draw her close, details can be a powerful ally. For there are some things that the gruffest buffalo does well to be aware of. Butterflies need to be noticed. A wise man keeps his eyes open. It's good for me to know that Tami's favorite flower is freesia, her favorite author is Karen Kingsbury, her favorite perfume is Lauren Style, and her favorite Chinese food is sweet-and-sour chicken. All these details are part of who Tami is. To show her she's important, I need to focus on them. They might be little things, but like a cotter pin that holds a wheel together, little things can be important.

So when Tami wants a coffee drink, I order a single decaf nonfat vanilla latte without foam.

If *I* can remember all those details, there's definitely hope for men.

TRANSLATION GUIDE

Men: Her attention to detail means "Life is meaningful because of its beauty and intricacy."

Women: His focus on the big picture means "Life is meaningful because of its structure and direction."

Both are right!

---

1. What important details does he always seem to miss?
2. What big picture considerations does she seem to forget?
3. Why are both the details and the big picture important?

SIXTEEN

Let the Games Begin

Boys will be boys.

I just spent an afternoon with my two teenage boys. I want them to connect and be best friends. Dylan and Dustin can sometimes get along great. But not today. Even as we were having fun together, they wouldn't stop fighting. Throughout the afternoon, everything became a competition.

Who's faster?

Who's stronger?

Who's smarter?

Who's right?

Who's best?

They'd fight, argue, wrestle, and harass each other. My boys love each other. They're just being boys. Little men.

Men like competition. They like to win. They want to be in control. They want to be strong. They tend to be more physical and aggressive. This is one reason men enjoy sports, either as participants or as spectators. They want to be champions, warriors at the top of the heap. Men tend to be more into accomplishment, achievement, proving superiority. To summarize John Eldredge in *Wild at Heart*, men have an innate, God-given drive to:

1. Fight a battle.
2. Discover an adventure.
3. Rescue a beauty.

Men are protectors and providers, explorers and risk takers. This is just the way men are. To suppress these drives and feminize a man is to diminish his identity and undermine his purpose. This frequently leaves a man bored, depressed, angry, and emotionally confused. A man needs to be a man. But this is absolutely *not* an excuse for him to be:

- rude
- insensitive
- cruel
- abusive
- harsh
- demanding
- hurtful

A man can be strong and masculine without exhibiting any of these qualities.

Competitiveness and strength can serve men well in many areas, but they also have significant downsides. Men can get into a win-at-all-costs mentality that can lead to compulsivity, perfectionism, and burnout at work. They can get so wrapped up in competition that they sabotage themselves by risking too much, getting out of balance, or creating unnecessary conflicts. Men need to realize that everything in life is not a competition.

Women may also enjoy competition, but they tend to see it differently than men. Women often use competition as a means to increase connection. Winning may be just as important to them, but their mentality has a social-relational component. When Brittany, my daughter, was in high school, she was on the soccer team for two years. She was an aggressive player, and she and her teammates wanted to win, but they also wanted to have fun with one another. They would talk and joke, spend the night at one another's homes, go shopping together, and celebrate one another's birthdays. Competition was important, but connection was equally important.

In contrast, when Dusty plays soccer, his head is totally into the game. Winning is everything, even if he has to harass his own teammates. It's the game that's important, not the relationships. In fact, there are still members of his team whose names he doesn't know. I asked him about this, and he told me, "Names aren't important; I know all the positions they're playing, though."

When husbands or wives bring competition into their home lives, tensions can build rapidly. It can lead husbands to become heavy-handed and demanding and women to become controlling and critical. Men are designed with a desire to be strong leaders, and in marriage they often compete to maintain their position. They are also culturally trained that it is "unmanly" to hold a weak position. For the sake of their self-esteem, they will fight, using any method possible, to win this competition.

Women, on the other hand, fight in order to fulfill their need to feel secure. If they feel insecure, unloved, disregarded, threatened, or taken advantage of, they too can move into a competitive stance. They do this not to win as a man would, but to protect themselves. They may also do this to gain a sense of value in their husbands' eyes or to achieve an equal footing on which the two of them might connect.

For women, everything doesn't have to be a race or a competition. Women can play a game without having to win, have a conversation without having to be right, or take a hike without having to finish first. In fact, a woman will avoid winning too much with either her friends or her husband in the interest of harmony and goodwill. A woman would rather orchestrate a win-win situation than a win-lose one, even if she would be the winner. For as she deals with her husband, she realizes that if her husband loses, she frequently loses too because of the hit on his self-esteem. This is especially true if he loses to her on a regular basis. Then he is likely to create more conflicts with her (in an attempt to eventually win) or withdraw from her (to avoid humiliation) or have an affair (so he can find another venue in which to win). As someone I know once said, "Sometimes when you lose, you win." Jesus said something very similar: "If anyone wants to be first, he must be the very last, and the servant of all" (Mark 9:35). Now that's an interesting take on competition.

If a woman feels disconnected from her husband in any way, she might use playful—or serious—competition as a strategy to get him to notice her and so to open up the doors to communication and connection.

It can also be fun and positive to compete together as a team against individuals or forces outside the marriage. In such a situation a couple become allies in a competition beyond themselves. They protect, defend, encourage, help, and challenge each other to achieve a mutual win.

Still, though competition might strongly benefit a relationship, to build a healthy, long-lasting marriage, connection is the real goal. Women's viewpoint in this area is usually the healthiest.

Women need to recognize that competition in men is just a part of who they are. Women should not be offended by it or try to shut it down. Men, on the other hand, need to make sure that their competitive side does not hinder their closeness at home. Men need to recognize that women often see gentleness as more manly than gruffness.

As a kid, I loved three-legged races, where two people stood side by side, their inner legs tied together. To win this race, you had to place your arm around the other's shoulders and move your outer legs forward at the same time. Those who did best were the ones who competed wholeheartedly by working *together* in connected unity.

Life is frequently a competition, and each couple is a team—both partners on the same side. If you lose your connection and start to compete antagonistically against each other, you both end up flat on your faces. But if both of you compete for each other's love, against all threats and barriers, then you will ultimately enjoy the satisfaction of a great connection. You both win.

Competition and connection don't have to be opposing forces; they just have to be carefully coordinated.

Hey, wanna arm-wrestle?

TRANSLATION GUIDE

Women: His competitiveness means "My success as provider and protector means I have to win."

Men: Her desire for connection means "We need to be a team so that together we can defeat the influences that would undermine us."

1. In what areas does he like to compete?
2. What are her favorite ways to make connection?
3. How can the two of you connect in order to compete as a team?

SEVENTEEN

Partner or Parent?

Y ou're not my father."

"Don't mother me!"

Have you ever said something like this to your spouse? Or heard it from your spouse?

Nobody wants to be parented by one's spouse. It's demeaning and offensive. After all, we are adults. We outgrew our parents years ago.

Or did we? Maybe rather than outgrowing them, we *became* them. As a child I saw certain things my father did that I swore I'd never do. But now I'm doing those very things—sometimes to my wife. The older we get, the more likely we are to take on the traits of our same-sex parent.

The parent trap sneaks up on us from the other direction too. Nobody wants to be married to one's opposite-sex parent, no matter how great a parent he or she might be. Yet at times that's exactly the sort of person we marry or expect our spouse to be more like. If a woman's father was hard-working or good with money or incredibly patient, that's what she expects from a husband. If a man's mother was a good cook or athletic or very optimistic, that's what he expects from a wife. We take all the positive attributes of our opposite-sex parent and assume a good spouse should have those traits. If they don't, we're disappointed and feel cheated or deceived in some way.

But here's the problem: at the same time, we take all the negative traits of our opposite-sex parent and assume that a good spouse should have *none* of these.

Our parents were important figures in our lives, and like it or not, we are constantly living in their shadows. But this is not all bad.

Healthy fathers provide and protect. As providers, they gave us stable environments where our basic needs of food and shelter were met. They also provided emotional security so we were free to relax, have fun, and grow. As protectors, they did their best to ward off danger—anything that threatened our security. They gave us strength and courage and confidence. When Dad was around, we felt safe.

These are father gifts that most women also expect, at some level, out of their husbands. In fact most wives want their husbands to do at least as well as their fathers did in these areas and hopefully better. Women want their husbands to be as strong as their fathers, but also to be as sensitive as their mothers. It's an interesting blend that most men find difficult to achieve. Still, a woman's father sets the minimum standards for providing and protecting by which she expects her husband to prove his love to and for her.

Healthy mothers nurture and comfort. As nurturers they were full of encouraging and affirming words. They gave us warm environments where we knew we were always loved, even when we didn't feel very lovable or didn't deserve it. They gave us softness and sensitivity when the world seemed cold and cruel and callous. As comforters, they were always there. When we were sick, hurt, hungry, frustrated, depressed, or discouraged, Mom could somehow make us feel better.

These are mother gifts that most men also expect, at some level, out of their wives. If a man's wife is not as compassionate as his mother, he will frequently see her as unfeminine and challenging to his masculinity. Yet while men want their wives to be as tender and gentle as their mothers, they also want them to be strong like their fathers to handle life's pressures without falling apart. If, however, a woman appears too strong, her husband might see her as a competitor rather than a companion. Men might not always admit it, since it's not politically correct, but they're often attracted to women who are able to express their soft side. After all, that's what Mom did.

Most women like to be provided for and protected, while most men like to be nurtured and comforted. But no spouse likes to be parented. It's belittling and disrespectful. As adults we need to be treated as adults, not as children. Yet I frequently hear two complaints. Women usually give me...

The Kid Complaint

"He acts like one of the kids; in fact, he acts worse than the kids."

Of course he does. What's the problem? Every man has a boy inside who likes to play, take risks, and even be a little crazy. This is how he reduces his stress and connects with his kids (and sometimes his friends). Let him be, unless he is truly getting out of control.

Meanwhile men usually give me...

The Competency Complaint

"If I don't tell her exactly what to do, she'll get it all wrong."

Come on, let's be honest. What he's really saying is "My way is the best way, the right way, the only way, the most efficient way, or the way I prefer." Relax. She's an intelligent human being, and she'll figure it out. If she needs help, she'll ask. (Unlike most men. But that's another chapter.) Besides, if she does it all wrong, it probably won't be the end of the world.

Whichever complaint is yours, keep in mind: becoming parental with your spouse will *not* strengthen your marriage.

In a healthy marriage, spouses keep their roles straight. Husbands need to be husbands, not fathers; wives need to be wives, not mothers. If one spouse starts acting parental, the other spouse may resort to one of the following unhealthy defense strategies:

1. **Starting a fight.** You may stir up an intense power struggle—as you might have done when your parents offended you—usually over something totally stupid.

2. **Building a wall.** The feelings of belittlement can be so painful that you withdraw to heal. Your spouse no longer feels safe, and you build a wall of resentment.

3. **Acting like a kid.** You tell yourself that if your spouse is going to treat you like a kid, you might as well fulfill his or her expectations.

4. **Looking elsewhere.** When you feel disrespected and pushed away, you may be tempted to look to someone besides your spouse to fill the void.

Each of these is dangerous and potentially destructive to your relationship.

Now, the parent trap presents yet one more challenge to many couples. This involves our openness to each other. Sometimes we stubbornly want to be in control. When we were children, our parents had control. As adults, we resist what feels like our spouses' control; it reminds us too much of our past. It's easy to then resort to two passive-aggressive strategies:

- *We can't always hear truth from our spouses.* In fact, frequently we can hear truth from almost *anybody else.* We disbelieve and argue with our spouses' perceptions or opinions, but we listen intently to the same thoughts from a friend.

- *We can't always accept help from our spouses.* Offers of help from our partners can feel controlling or like statements about our competency. We want to prove that we can do it ourselves. Yet a friend's offer seems generous and caring.

When we resist each other in either of these ways, we're really still trying to prove our independence from our parents.

We're all drawn to the familiar. There are bound to be similarities between our parents and our spouses. That's just the way it is. Parents can be wonderful, but they have a specific role in our lives. Parents set an *example* of adult maturity and a healthy marriage. Parents set our *expectations* of what each spouse should do. Parents also shape our *fears* of what is unhealthy in a marriage and the negative patterns we definitely want to avoid. Yet we must beware that unresolved issues with our parents can slip into our marriages.

So treat each other lovingly and kindly. Women, do not smother or mother your husbands, no matter how much they seem to need it. Men, do not control or command your wives; be tender toward them, not paternal.

Treat each other respectfully. Being parented once is truly enough.

CHAPTER SUMMARY

We naturally look to our spouse to provide the gifts we used to receive from our opposite-sex parent. But taken too far, the "parenting" of one spouse by the other is unhealthy and demeaning.

1. How does your spouse remind you of either of your parents?
2. Which of the four unhealthy patterns on page 89 are you most likely to resort to when your spouse acts parental?
3. In what areas is it most difficult to hear truth from your spouse?

EIGHTEEN

The Distance Between Two Points

W e can make the trip in a day."

"No we can't," insisted Tami.

That was all the challenge I needed. "I think we can do this."

"But it's over 950 miles, and we have a four-month-old infant," Tami tried patiently to explain.

So what? I thought. But I'd learned long ago not to say what I think. Instead I sensitively said, "If we get too tired, we can always stop and get a motel." Yet in my head I persisted: *We can do this! What a great challenge!*

Off we went. My eyes were set on the finish line. I focused on the road, constantly calculating how many miles we had left and how many hours it would take to reach our destination. The race was on.

Tami didn't understand the importance of the race. She wanted to slow down to look at the landscape or watch the birds circle overhead. She wanted to take a quick side trip. She even wanted to take bathroom breaks and food stops. She just didn't get it. Road trip efficiency demanded that we combine gas, food, and bathroom breaks all into one stop. We couldn't waste time. We had a goal to reach, a challenge to conquer. Nothing was going to slow me down.

I was being a man. Tami was being a woman. Neither of us was completely right or wrong.

Men like to stay on task. They want to go from point A to point B as quickly and economically as possible. Men hate distractions and obstacles. They are driven, obsessed, focused. They bulldoze through difficulties so they can get to the destination. Only then can they relax. Women are more likely to enjoy the journey and may even be disappointed when it's over. They see distractions and obstacles as acceptable or even enjoyable aspects of life—opportunities for connection and conversation.

For men, the destination is the task, and they tolerate the journey as a necessary evil. For women, the journey is the task, and it should be relaxing, positive, and as long as it takes.

Women see a journey as a chance to enhance and deepen the marriage relationship. The journey is an escape from the pressures of everyday life, a time to be alone with their husbands, a setting in which to demonstrate care and affirmation.

While men like to keep on track, women love to explore the side roads. To men, side roads are confusing and a waste of time. How will anything ever get done without steady progress toward the goal? To women, side roads might be the best part of the journey. They add atmosphere, something more to talk about, new ways to build a relationship. Women are elevating relational values; men are elevating direct, accomplishment-focused values.

Observe the journey-destination contrast at work in a simple phone conversation. When I call someone, I get right to business. "This is what I want" or "This is what I need to know." The other person responds, I say thanks, and the conversation is over in a few minutes. If someone calls me, I might ask, "How can I help you?" or "Is there something you need?" I want to get directly to the point.

Tami would never ask such questions. She can talk on the phone for hours—or so it seems to me. After one such conversation, I asked what she'd been talking about so long.

"Oh, nothing."

"What do you mean, 'nothing'?"

"I can't remember exactly what we talked about, but it was a great conversation." She smiled contentedly.

This doesn't make any sense to men. Women don't mind beating around the bush; bush-beating is a great frustration to most men. For women, the conversation itself is the goal since it promotes connection. Men talk for a purpose, to get to a destination. For women talk is a journey—the longer and more convoluted, the better. They enjoy the trip. And when they reach the destination—when they end the conversation—they may feel sad. Their connection is ending, at least temporarily, and they must get back to all the everyday chores that have been waiting for them.

Men who become single-channeled and focused only on the goal miss wonderful opportunities to draw closer to their wives. Showing love along the way is usually more important than when and how fast you get there. If the journey tears you apart, the destination usually becomes irrelevant.

Yet women who seldom if ever think about the destination—or who inadvertently hinder their husbands from actively accomplishing their goals—will discover disappointment and sometimes disaster when tasks men believe are important are not completed carefully, correctly, or on time.

Let me encourage men to not be so focused on the destination that we make the trip miserable. And let me encourage women to be patient with men, realizing that they don't mean to ignore you, invalidate you, drive you crazy, or run you over on their way to that all-important finish line. They're trying to do something good, often for you and your family.

In the end, both priorities are important. So enjoy your trip. But make sure you arrive at the destination together.

TRANSLATION GUIDE

Women: His focus on the destination means "It's important to get the job done."

Men: Her focus on the journey means "It's important to enjoy the process."

Both are right!

---

1. In what ways is she process- or journey-oriented?
2. In what ways is he goal- or destination-oriented?
3. How do the two of you cope with these differences?
4. When is the last time these differences got in your way?

NINETEEN

Oh, One More Thing...

A woman's work is never done. There's always more to do.

"Tami, just sit down and relax." I pat the seat beside me on the couch.

"I can't," she says. "There's laundry and dishes and vacuuming and hundreds of other things that I have to get to."

"But it's okay," I try to explain. "Relax tonight, and you can do all those other things tomorrow."

"You don't understand. I can't relax. If I put things off till tomorrow, I'll have twice as much to do."

"Just sit down beside me for a little while. Let's watch TV together."

A long pause. "Okay." Reluctantly she sits by me. A few minutes later she's back up and bustling about—checking on the laundry, talking on the phone, doing the dishes, making a grocery list, *and* watching TV.

"Tami, could you please sit down?" I plead. "Just watching you is making me tired." As she rejoins me, she doesn't see me shaking my head at her persistent busyness. But I do notice her shaking her head about my interference with her work.

Women are amazing. They have this incredible ability to multitask.

They're like master jugglers who can keep five or six objects in the air simultaneously. Men tend to focus on one task at a time. They start with a single objective and stick with it until it's finished. Then they move on to the next job. If men are forced to multitask, they can keep it up for short periods of time. But it doesn't come naturally, and they rarely do it as well as their wives (though this is hard for most men to admit).

When my children were toddlers, Tami would often leave for a few hours and ask me to watch the kids. Now, this sounds easier than it really is. If I would put everything else down and focus on the kids, it was no problem. But I usually had another project I was working on. So I'd try to do both. I usually thought I was doing pretty good—that is, until Tami came home and started asking unreasonable questions. Questions like…

"Where are the kids?"

"I heard them in the next room." *Don't worry. I'm on top of it.*

"When did they get into the closet?"

"I don't know."

"Why did you let them color on the wall?"

"Uh, I'm not sure about that either."

"What did you feed them for lunch?"

"Oh, I guess I forgot about that. But they were having a great time."

At this point, Tami would shake her head and walk away. By then I'd realized that I hadn't fulfilled my assignment as well as I thought I had, but multitasking doesn't come naturally to men. We have to work at it. To be honest, though, a lot of times we don't try hard enough.

Men want to focus 100 percent of their attention on one and only one thing while shutting out everything else. A man can be watching TV, reading a book, or working on a project, and be oblivious to everything else that's happening around him. The house can be burning down, his wife can be calling him for the hundredth time, but he can stay unwaveringly on task. He's simply being single-channeled. That's the way God made him.

Women also focus on multiple *thoughts* simultaneously. Their minds are constantly going—thinking about troubles, worries, emotions, relationships, plans, questions to ask, things to do, and a hundred other concerns. A woman commonly feels as if she's carrying the weight of the world on her shoulders...as if her brain is running at full speed and she can't turn it off. Even at the end of the day, when she desperately wants to relax or go to sleep, a woman often finds that her brain won't slow down. The Off switch seems to be broken.

Men don't usually have this problem, unless they get highly stressed. When they come home from work or are ready for sleep, they simply turn off their brains and stop thinking. They can lock up unwanted thoughts and emotions and pretend they don't exist. It's easy and natural for most men to sit back and literally think about nothing. That's how they unwind.

Women don't *want* to be preoccupied and driven by their multitude of thoughts and emotions. But they are, and they often can't help it. This doesn't make sense to most men. We try to be helpful with counsel like:

- "Just let it go."
- "Stop thinking about it."
- "Don't let it bother you."
- "It's all going to be okay."

These sorts of statements frustrate most women, who would love to turn off their brains.

Early this morning, about two o'clock, Tami woke up with her mind racing. For an hour she made mental lists; planned out events for the next week; remembered three or four tasks she had forgotten; and worried about the kids, finances, and her father's health. Meanwhile, I slept soundly, unaware that there was a single problem in the world.

Women multitask because they think too much. They are constantly thinking and rethinking what they should do. Then they remember one more thing. Then another. They want to make sure everything works out just right because they don't want to disappoint anyone. As one woman once told me, "If I don't think about it, who will?"

After they've finished a task, men don't think about it anymore, unless something goes obviously and terribly wrong. Even if something doesn't turn out quite right, no worries. They figure they'll just fix it when they get a chance to.

Men don't go looking for additional tasks. In fact, frequently they don't even see tasks that are right in front of them. These tasks are so blatantly obvious to most women that they have a hard time believing men actually don't see them. So women become baffled and frustrated when men don't address something that's right under their noses. Women then accuse men of being blind, lazy, selfish, or insensitive. But this isn't fair. They're just being men. They're doing something; but for them, that one thing is all that exists in their world.

Many men like lists. They can work through these neatly and orderly. When one item is completed, they cross it out and move to the next. They don't look ahead or behind. Women use lists, too, but in a totally different way. They work on multiple items simultaneously, jumping from one to another in no particular order. When they finish an item, they don't necessarily check it off; they're not absolutely sure it's done as completely or as well as it should be, so they keep open the option of going back to it in the future. This drives men crazy. They want to lean over and check things off their wives' lists. How else are their wives going to know that something's done so they can relax? And how are their wives going to know when the whole list is done so they can crumple it up and throw it away? Women rarely throw away their lists. They add to and revise and update their lists. No wonder a woman's work is never done.

Lately I've been trying to move beyond being single-channeled, and I think it's working. I don't think I'll ever be able to multitask as well as Tami does, but I *am* learning to double-task. When I'm focused on something and Tami comes into the room, I try to acknowledge her. When I'm watching TV (task #1), I put my arm around her (part of task #2). And when a commercial comes on, I tell her I love her (completion of task #2). This double-tasking is quite a challenge, but it's also a lot of fun.

In fact, I've learned that while doing almost anything, I can also at the same time reach out and somehow let Tami know...

- that I truly appreciate her.
- how special she is.
- how much I love her.

I guess there really is hope for us guys.

TRANSLATION GUIDE

Men: Her multitasking means "It's truly hard for me to rest when so many tasks await me; I can't forget them."

Women: His single-channeling means "I feel overwhelmed and paralyzed when I'm faced with too many tasks at one time."

1. In what ways does she regularly multitask?
2. When was the last time he got stuck on a single channel?
3. What are the advantages and disadvantages of each of these styles?

TWENTY

Decent Exposure

We were driving home from a wonderful weekend at the beach when Tami cornered me. "Why don't men apologize?" she asked.

My defenses shot up. "We do."

"Then why don't *you* apologize?" Several uncomfortable seconds of silence followed. Then Tami proceeded to enumerate a number of offenses for which she thought I should apologize.

And she was right.

I inhaled deeply. Then purged my lungs. And apologized.

Lightning didn't strike and the world didn't end. Nothing terrible happened.

As we neared home, Tami said, "Did you notice that you've apologized more in the last half hour than during our entire marriage?"

I almost said something. I wanted to defend myself, to invalidate her statement. I wanted to argue. But a moment of sanity gripped me, and I kept my mouth shut.

Instead I put that defensive energy to work pondering the question: why do most women find it easy and natural to apologize, while most men find it so hard?

Since then I've figured out that women don't mind apologizing because it's one of their methods of connecting. They see apologies as positive—opportunities to take responsibility and share their troubles. Tami seems to tell everybody her frustrations and feelings. This is her way of working through them and strengthening her support system. Vulnerability triggers compassion and companionship from her friends. Thus she feels closer to these friends and better about her troubles. An apology solves a problem.

But to men, an apology *spotlights* a problem. Men see apologies as negative, making them appear weak or casting them in a bad light. Men are taught to protect themselves at all costs. They believe they always need to be strong, right, in control. They believe, rightly or wrongly, that exposure will put them in a one-down position and people will think less of them or take advantage of them. So they hide their mistakes, weaknesses, and failures. They cover it all with an "everything's great" facade. To apologize means exposing the fact that they don't have it all together.

Now, a wife can already see through her husband's facade. She knows better than anyone else his mistakes, weaknesses, and failures. She wants him to be open and honest with her, to trust her. But men struggle to trust anybody. They're taught from early in life that everybody will sooner or later let you down, so the only one to trust is oneself. Therefore men build walls around their hearts and avoid talking about anything that is too...

- personal
- painful
- embarrassing
- emotional
- relational
- overwhelming

- confusing
- self-effacing

Apologizing usually involves exposing these areas. Even though most men love their wives, the risks associated with apologizing feel too great. They'll do almost anything to avoid vulnerability, even if it means enduring excruciating emotional pain.

You want to talk pain? Imagine Tim's. His wife left him for another man. Tim was in shock. He loved his wife, and the betrayal cut deep. Tim met with a group of great guys every week to challenge and encourage each other. These guys had met regularly for several years and were close. Three weeks after Tim's wife left, I asked him how he was doing.

"Not good," he answered.

"Are the guys in your group there for you?" I asked.

"I haven't said anything to them yet."

"Why not?"

"It's just too embarrassing," he said. "Besides, I didn't want to bother them with my problems."

Many men would rather die than lose face. But their faulty assumption that an apology means losing face is based in part on their belief that...

- if I did bad, I must be bad.
- if I failed, I must be a failure.

Men tend to generalize a single event into a statement of character. Therefore to apologize is to announce that one is bad or a failure. Most men realize that this is irrational, but it's still how they think.

If only they would realize that talking about a failure or weakness can make them feel better...and make them *look* better in the eyes of their wives. When a wife sees her husband being vulnerable or apologizing, she sees it as a strength—as honesty and responsibility and caring. Then she feels closer and loves him more. In contrast, when a husband doesn't apologize, his wife sometimes feels rejected or minimized, pushed away or taken for granted. One woman told me, "If he really loved me, he'd say he's sorry." But if a man has a hard time acknowledging his failure to himself, he may not even recognize the need to apologize to someone else.

In any relationship, an apology can soften a heart, build a bond, heal a wound, or generate hope. Every one of us needs to apologize periodically. (Yes, Tami, I really am writing this.) A marriage is like a dance, and even in the best relationships people step on each other's toes. This is usually unintentional, but that's not the point. Anything that one partner does that puts stress on the relationship needs to be acknowledged and dealt with. Ask yourself the following questions to determine if you have something for which you should say "I'm sorry":

1. Have I been wrong (even if just partially)?
2. Have I been rude or insensitive?
3. Have I been defensive or deceptive?
4. Have I been impatient or pushy?
5. Have I been negative, critical, or demeaning?
6. Have I acted hurtfully (accidentally or intentionally)?
7. Have I forgotten, neglected, ignored, or overlooked something important to my spouse?
8. Have I damaged or misused something that's not mine (even if it was an accident)?

Even though women are naturally better at apologies, that doesn't let men off the hook. We men need to step out, swallow our pride, and take the risk of vulnerability.

As for women, they need to recognize how difficult this is for men and not use men's honesty against them. Women also need to be care-ful to not demand apologies from their husbands; many men interpret this as being asked to grovel. Instead, women can gracefully nudge their husbands by saying something like:

- "Maybe I'm being hypersensitive, but that hurt."
- "Your words or actions often have a lot more impact on me than you might be aware."
- "Did you realize you forgot something that's important to me?"

I know men often don't get hints, and these lines certainly aren't as direct as they could be. But sometimes an indirect approach does work better. So, men, watch for ways your wives might be nudging you toward an apology.

I'd also encourage women to understand that men are more apt to apologize in practical, nonverbal ways. This might not be a female's pre-ferred method, but it's still valid. A nonverbal apology can be as genuine and heartfelt as something verbalized—sometimes more so. A verbal "I'm sorry" can be a meaningless ritual if done simply to appease a spouse or to shut them up. Nonverbal apologies can be a wonderful means of taking responsibility and showing love. So please do not dis-miss or marginalize gestures like giving flowers, planning a date, doing special chores, being playful, or initiating romance. Each of these can be ways of saying, "I'm sorry. I love you. Are we okay?" Please accept them as a man's sincere attempts to acknowledge his guilt.

At certain times apologies can be difficult for both husbands and wives. Who hurt whom? Who hurt whom first? Who hurt whom the deepest? Who holds the greatest responsibility? Sometimes the apology war reaches a stalemate, both partners stubbornly holding out for the other to make the first move. How do you break through this emotional blockade? Emerson Eggerichs, in his classic *Love & Respect*, suggests that the first move of reconciliation should be made by "the one who sees himself or herself as the most mature." For men, this transforms an apology from an affirmation of weakness (associated with shame and failure) to an affirmation of strength (associated with maturity and love).

Apologies may be awkward and difficult. They may feel humiliating. But an apology is one of the most powerful ways to build trust and intimacy. Sincere apologies can heal hurts and resolve conflicts. Though an apology often feels like indecent exposure, it's usually the most *decent* thing you can do.

TRANSLATION GUIDE

Men: Her desire for apologies means "I feel distant from you when something unresolved stands between us."

Women: His resistance to verbal apologies means "I feel like a failure when I admit I did something wrong; but I can *show* you I'm sorry."

1. What were the circumstances the last time either of you apologized?
2. When is it hardest for either of you to apologize?
3. In what nonverbal ways do you sometimes apologize?

TWENTY-ONE

Deleting and Scrapbooking

Tami's leaving tomorrow for a scrapbooking weekend. She and her girlfriends are going to the mountains with a car full of photographs. I'm not sure what exactly they do on these all-girl, no-guys-allowed getaways, but Tami comes back excited and energized. Somehow the process of going through old pictures—labeling them, talking about them, gluing them into books, and whatever else—is a positive experience. And somehow I come out a winner in this situation. When she comes home, she has missed me and is often romantically appreciative that I encouraged her to go. So in the end, we're both happy.

Most women love to scrapbook. They can look at a photo and suddenly be transported back to the very day it was taken. They become absorbed in the details and emotions of that moment, savoring it with a joy that leaves most men baffled. Men look at the same picture and vaguely recognize it. They appreciate the memory, but men live in the present. Pictures are special and meaningful, but they don't usually hold for men the same emotional fullness they do for women.

Women scrapbook the past. Events that hold intense emotions, positive or negative, are carefully stored away to be brought back at a moment's notice. Many people insist that women never forget. This is what reinforces and enriches the deep, emotional landscape of a woman's world.

Men frequently delete the past. They'll keep memories for a while. But if they don't appear useful, relevant, or consistent with their present needs and worldview, they're dumped in the mental round file.

About a year ago Tami and I were reminiscing about our early married days, and Tami said, "It's hard to believe you were so rude."

I was surprised by the statement and asked her what she meant. Tami then reminded me that when we were first married we had only one car and worked at the same place.

"Yes," I said. I remembered that very clearly.

But then she went on to tell me that, because I started work an hour later than her and "needed my sleep," I made her ride the bus alone to work rather than make the extra fifteen-minute trip to drop her off. That situation went on for about six months.

And I don't have even one memory of it.

I have searched my memory trying to find even the faintest recollection of what she said happened. But I can find nothing. If Tami wasn't such a truthful person, I would say she fabricated the memory. But I know that isn't the case. It's embarrassing for me to admit how selfish and insensitive I was, but it's also disturbing how effectively I could delete a memory that must have been repeated about a hundred times. Yet, like most couples, Tami scrapbooked and I deleted.

This pattern of dealing with the past frequently gets couples into deep trouble. As women scrapbook, they are reminded of all the selfish, insensitive, foolish, hurtful things their husbands have done. Every time they review the pages of their mental scrapbooks, those negative memories jump out at them, intensifying the original hurts and keeping them alive. As more pages are added, soon she has a sizable backlog of painful events stored and regularly reviewed. Interestingly, the negative memories are more distinctively highlighted, and if she isn't careful, they tend to overshadow the positive memories.

Meanwhile, men tend to fairly quickly delete the negative memories, especially if they are:

- embarrassing
- self-incriminating
- belittling
- confusing
- unfixable

Then they move on as if those events never happened.

These two contrasting patterns of dealing with negative memories might not be a problem if the positives always outweighed the negatives. But in most marriages there are times when something upsets the scales. During these times women can easily come across (to men) as stirring up trouble, while men appear (to women) to be minimizing reality.

Yet scrapbooking and deleting both have their own significant advantages, as well as disadvantages. Scrapbooking allows women to track troubles and their patterns; these can then be synthesized into diagnoses and, hopefully, helpful prescriptions for repair. Yet negatively focused scrapbooking can also make women critical, bitter, and unforgiving. Then they can lose hope, move into depression, and alienate their husbands.

Deleting allows men to be positive and optimistic, without getting dragged into the negatives that can be deadly to relationships. Deleting can keep one from digging into yesterday's garbage. It keeps short accounts and is quick to forgive. But it can also create blind spots to growing difficulties. Men are frequently naive about situations until they blow up in their faces. This lack of data keeps them from being able to fix problems or at least control the damage. It also can cause men to minimize their wives' concerns, thinking they're overreacting or man-ufacturing problems. Wives then don't feel taken seriously, which increases their negative feelings and gives them one more thing to scrap-book.

When challenges and frustrations hit a marriage—and they inevitably will—these two responses frequently collide. Women scrap-book, extensively examining each problem in the belief that thinking and talking about an issue will lead to its resolution. Men delete; they erase all memory of the issue, in the belief that thinking and talking about an issue is what turns it into a problem. In their minds, ignoring it actually resolves it.

Both systems are flawed. The answer is some type of middle ground, which is neither negative nor naive. Scrapbooking, at its worst, is pessimistic and hopeless. While deleting, at its worst, is dishonest and dangerously optimistic.

What if men were to try their hand at minimal scrapbooking? And what if women were to take a shot at periodic deleting? If each partner used a combination of styles, the advantages and disadvantages might just balance out. A man doesn't mind scrapbooking the positives, but he should hold on to some of the negatives—in particular, those for which he is responsible and those that are particularly bothersome to his wife. Don't focus on *her* negatives, attempting to fix her. A man should choose to keep photos that remind him what *he* needs to apologize for and where he needs to seek improvement. This affirms his wife and gives her hope. It also allows him to learn from the past, so he can build a better future.

Likewise women desperately need to delete. Many have scrap-booked far too many negative pictures and won't let go of them. Sure, her husband has done stupid, insensitive things; I'm not defending his actions. But endlessly reviewing some of those pictures accomplishes nothing worthwhile and overshadows the positive pictures in the scrapbook. Sometimes the best thing to do is to forgive him, tear up the old pictures, and press the Delete button. He may not deserve it, but hasn't he deleted a lot of the stupid, insensitive things *you've* done? (Now, if you honestly can't delete certain pictures and they're undermining your marriage, please talk to a pastor, priest, counselor, or psychologist about it.)

"So that's why she gets so frustrated with me," George said when I explained scrapbooking and deleting.

"And that's why I was so upset at you yesterday when you didn't follow the grocery list," Jan insisted.

He turned to her in surprise. "I didn't know you were upset at me."

"Why do you think we were fighting?"

"I don't know." He looked perplexed.

"You see, it's just like Dr. Steve said." Jan looked exasperated. "But you delete so fast that you can't even remember deleting."

TRANSLATION GUIDE

Men: Her accumulation of negative memories means "It's very hard for me to let go of something painful."

Women: His forgetfulness of past offenses means "I survive emotionally by quickly letting go of negative experiences."

1. What sort of things is she most likely to scrapbook about the relationship? Give examples.
2. What sort of things is he most likely to delete about the relationship? Give examples.
3. How do scrapbooking and deleting in your relationship create frustration or conflict?

TWENTY-TWO

Sticks and Stones...
and Words

W hy can't you do anything right?" Sandi looked in disgust at the plate.

"I made you your favorite sandwich," Phillip said.

"And you're really proud of yourself, aren't you? Do you know how many sandwiches I've made for you? Besides, I asked for just a little mustard. Look at this." She opened the sandwich. "Does this look like a little mustard?"

Phillip stared wordlessly at the huge glob of mustard. What could he say? He'd tried to do something nice, but he'd blown it. Maybe he hadn't listened. Maybe he'd been too hurried. Maybe he'd forgotten. For whatever reason, he'd done it wrong, and his wife was unhappy.

Men desperately want to please their wives.

It's true. They would do almost anything to make their wives happy. But sadly, many men have given up.

Some men have come to the conclusion that satisfying their wives' needs and desires is impossible. No matter what they attempt, some mistake always seems to invalidate their good intentions. So why try?

Men want to win their wives, but too many times their efforts seem to make the situation worse. Many men have resigned themselves to their wives' seasons of grumpiness and irritability. If a husband asks what's wrong, he becomes the focus of all her frustration. Then things escalate as she gripes, moans, attacks, complains, and nags. Most men don't know what to do, so they either fight back or withdraw. Both strategies tend to further deteriorate the relationship.

Now, I realize I'm being much harder on women at this point, but I don't think women realize how negative they can become. I don't think they do it on purpose. Maybe it's a combination of their focusing on the details, their scrapbooking, their exhaustion from multitasking, or their frustration because we guys don't seem to get it. But whatever the reason, negativity pushes men away. The number one reason men seek divorce is that they feel their wives are critical and they can't seem to make them happy. This corresponds to wives' number one complaint that their husbands don't listen and don't take them seriously. So men must learn to listen better, and women need to learn to be less critical.

Men and women handle negativity so differently. Women love to talk things through. So their real reasons for talking about negatives are to:

- vent and reduce inner pressure.
- raise awareness of a problem.
- resolve it together.
- gain agreement and consensus about it.

Talking about negative issues makes a woman feel better. What her husband sees as criticism is often simply her verbal processing. Her healthiest means of problem solving gets horribly lost in translation.

But the language barrier has two sides; women need to understand men too. Talking about negative issues makes men feel worse—uncomfortable and overwhelmed. Men do all they can to avoid talking about these issues; that's why they use deleting so much. When a wife sounds critical, a man usually feels like he's failed and he's just been put down. He responds very strongly to this—like he's been slugged in the gut—though he might never show it on the outside. He feels frustrated, upset at himself, and humiliated by his wife's "pointing finger." This is one more reminder: *I'm a bad husband. I can't do anything right. I can't even make my wife happy.* Hopelessness grabs his ankles and drags him down. He might lash out in defensiveness, or more often simply withdraw into shame and silence. Either response causes his wife to feel abandoned and insecure, so she accuses him of passive-aggressiveness or stonewalling. Not knowing how to respond, he withdraws even further.

Criticism cuts a husband faster and deeper than almost anything else. It pushes him away—into his work, hobbies, addictions, and deeper into himself. Sometimes even into the arms of another woman. A woman seldom realizes how much influence she has over her man's emotions. She can make or break him with a single sentence.

Men have this same potential influence over their wives. Criticism, even if it's said casually or in jest, can be a deadly weapon. Criticism can kill either spouse's...

- motivation
- enthusiasm
- confidence
- joy
- dreams
- hope
- spirit

But a man is especially prone to seeing criticism as rejection; it only reinforces his conviction that he can't make her happy.

When I shared this concept with a particular woman, she responded that maybe women wouldn't complain so much if there was nothing to complain about. I can't disagree with her. But I pointed out that criticism and complaints don't usually motivate men toward better behavior. What works best is encouragement and compliments.

Imagine if Sandi had said to Phillip, "Thank you so much for the sandwich. I really appreciate your effort, but next time would you go a little lighter on the mustard?" This sort of comment would get the point across to most husbands while motivating them to be more careful next time. A positive request will almost always get a better response than a negative comment. This might be why King Solomon wrote, "Better to live on a corner of the roof than share a house with a quarrelsome wife" (Proverbs 21:9). (I'm sure the same could be said of a complaining husband.)

Both husbands and wives have their negative moments, but positive compliments can compensate. Genuine compliments can be unifying, life-giving, marriage-enriching. A good compliment can turn my day around and make me feel great. It can uplift, energize, and comfort a spouse. The cure for criticism and complaints is compliments. If you can't think of a compliment, either you aren't thinking very hard or you're trapped deep in your own negativity. Complimenting is a skill that takes practice; the more you practice, the better you get.

Every day a couple should actively look for opportunities to compliment each other. As I compliment Tami, she becomes more positive and patient toward me. If I highlight her many strengths, she feels better about herself and ultimately feels better about me. The more often I compliment her, the better things get. So I'd be an idiot to not compliment her as often as I could.

But sometimes guys are idiots. We forget, are lazy, or become distracted. We love our wives, but we usually don't communicate that as clearly or consistently as we could. Consider the following four areas for compliments:

- **Appearance**: How does she look?
- **Actions**: What has he done?
- **Attitudes**: How does she think?
- **Attributes**: What is his character?

If I'd compliment Tami at least once every day in each of these four areas, she'd think I was a great husband. Complimenting a spouse in the first three of these is usually easy, but the fourth tends to take more thought. It's also the most powerful. To tell Tami how kind and patient and generous she is warms her heart, which then causes her to feel closer and more positive toward me. Which, in turn, makes her more kind and patient and generous. In the end, I'm usually the one who benefits most from these attributes.

Criticism kills. Compliments bring life. A healthy marriage provides a positive oasis in a desert of negativity. Compliments help by giving each other two amazing gifts.

1. *Uncommon safety.* No threatening, judging, or causing your spouse to feel uncomfortable. Encouraging them to be so relaxed in your presence that they feel safe enough to share their deepest hurt and loftiest dream.

2. *Unconditional positive regard.* Committing yourself to believing the very best about your mate without jumping to negative conclusions or looking for what's wrong. Instead, jumping to positive conclusions and searching with energetic determination for anything that is good.

When these two gifts are given daily, a relationship can grow and love can flourish. The antidote to criticism has been found, and negativity is forced to flee.

This is when Sandi picks up her sandwich and says, "Phillip, thank you. I'm so lucky you're my husband."

CHAPTER SUMMARY

Women need to talk out negative things in order to vent or resolve them; they often aren't accusing their husbands. Men tend to take these negative expressions personally and feel they've failed their wives; they sometimes despair of pleasing their wives. Both spouses can cure criticism with compliments.

1. When are either of you most likely to become critical of the other?
2. Which of you is best at compliments? Give each other three compliments sometime in the next twenty-four hours.
3. On a scale of 1 to 10, how would you rate yourselves on the two amazing gifts on page 117?

TWENTY-THREE

Why Won't He Talk?

Silence is golden. For men, that is.

And Drew was enjoying just that…a golden silent moment. He wasn't upset. He just needed to relax.

"What's wrong?" asked Carrie. "Are you feeling okay?"

"Everything's fine," he said. "I'm just enjoying some peace and quiet."

"Are you mad at me?"

"No." Drew laughed. "I'm just sitting and thinking."

"What are you thinking about?"

"Nothing."

"Why won't you talk to me?"

"I like to talk to you. But I don't have to talk all the time."

"Don't you understand that I talk to you because I love you, and I want us to have a great relationship?"

"I love you too." Drew was trying his best to stay calm. "But I don't necessarily have to talk about it."

"Are you sure nothing is bothering you?"

Why can't she respect my quiet? All I need is a little silence. Can't she just leave me alone for a little while? Drew took a deep breath. "For the tenth time, nothing is wrong. I promise. I'm not mad at you. I don't hate you. You're a beautiful woman. What else do I need to say for you just to relax and stop asking me all these questions?"

Carrie stepped back. "See, I knew something was wrong."

Drew shook his head, mumbled something under his breath, and walked out to the garage, slamming the door hard behind him.

Drew, like most men, loves peace and quiet. It calms his spirit and clears his head of all the clutter that collects there. He periodically needs silence like he needs his space. It gives him a chance to think, process, and try to figure things out. Or sometimes simply to unwind and day-dream about nothing in particular.

For Carrie, who can't turn off her brain, this concept of thinking about nothing is inconceivable. And to her, talk is valuable—essential!— in and of itself because it's the building material for closer relationships. But Drew talks only if he has to or if it achieves some objective. Why talk unless you have a good reason or some need for important data?

The more stressed a man is, the more he needs his silence. Talking sometimes seems to deepen his stress, highlighting the problems and enhancing the difficulties. His wife may come alongside him to help. To him, "helping" means being there to quietly support him with her mouth shut. But to her, it means talking about the cause of his stress. That is the last thing he wants. When everything is sorted out, he'll talk about it. But before that point, talk only adds pressure.

In the "language" of a woman, she needs to talk when she's stressed. It's her best method of problem solving. To keep silent about stress seems to increase its intensity. So she naturally believes that talking is what *he* needs and wants. To her, silence can be dangerous. But in his "language," silence is empowering.

It's hard to disagree with a woman's desire to connect with her husband through open, honest communication. Except that men naturally tend to be less verbal in most situations than their wives. Husbands are accused of refusing to communicate, and their wives frequently fear that they don't care about the relationship. I'm regularly asked, "How can I get my husband to talk to me?" Such a woman doesn't want to push him into the corner, put a gun to his head, and force him to talk. She just yearns to hear what's happened during his day and what's on his heart. She wants to break through his silence and recapture all the love and romance they enjoyed when they were dating. As one woman told me, "If he really loved me, he'd be excited about talking with me."

So why don't men talk more to their wives? They talk to co-workers, other guys, and total strangers but clam up with their wives. In fact, women often tell me that they learn more about their husbands when they listen to them talking to others than when the two of them talk alone.

Guys feel obligated to talk to others in order to compete in this crazy rat race of a world. (Remember, men are competitors.) To them, it's one of the essentials to being successful, saving face, proving themselves in public. But when they get home, they can relax and be themselves. The pressure's off. They don't have to perform. They can sit back and enjoy the quiet.

There are a lot of other reasons a man might not be talking. For example:

1. He doesn't know what to say.
2. He's processing the best answer.
3. He doesn't want to create conflict.
4. He doesn't want to intensify a situation (by disagreeing with or upsetting her).
5. He isn't sure how to articulate his position.

6. He's angry, hurt, or embarrassed.

7. He doesn't care about the subject matter.

8. He's overwhelmed by her talk or her amount of talk.

9. He's distracted.

10. He just wants to enjoy some silence.

To be totally honest, men sometimes use silence because it gives them more power. The more a woman pushes him to talk, the more his refusal reinforces his one-up position. This sort of passive-aggressive silence can undermine a relationship, making her insecure and anxious. (Now, wives, be very careful about accusing him of this, because if you aren't correct, you may push him even further into his silence.)

Another word for passive-aggressive silence is *stonewalling*—when a person won't respond or responds only with curt, one-word replies. The more she tries to break through this emotional wall, the more silent and distant he becomes, effectively shutting her down and pushing her away, leaving her feeling rejected, ignored, or devalued. John Gottman, in *Why Marriages Succeed or Fail*, discovered that 85 percent of husbands stonewall their wives during a conflict. Sometimes they actually do this for a positive reason—to calm themselves down so they don't blow up or say something they would later regret. But the result is often the less-than-positive cycle of his stonewalling, then her criticism, then more stonewalling, and so on. Therefore, another reason for silence might be a man's passive-aggressive response to his wife's negativity or criticism.

The whole dilemma stems from our childhood development. Females tend to develop verbal skills at an earlier age than males, so they tend to have confidence with talking that many men don't have. Therefore girls practice this verbal expression at a much higher rate than boys throughout their formative childhood and adolescent years.

Boys, meanwhile, tend to focus on areas in which they do well and to avoid areas in which they don't. So throughout their formative years, they miss out on more than a decade of practice. And even though men enter into adulthood fully capable of verbal communication, they've been conditioned to doubt their capability. If adult men believe that they don't do well expressing themselves verbally, especially regarding emotions or relationships, they tend to retreat to silence.

So how do women get their husbands to talk more? Here are a few ideas:

1. Talk with him, not at him.
2. Don't correct, criticize, or put him down.
3. Watch your tone of voice.
4. Keep it brief and to the point.
5. Ask for his opinion or perspective.
6. Listen to him.
7. Avoid interrupting.
8. Compliment him.
9. Beware of negativity or nagging.
10. Let him know how much you appreciate his input.

Also remember that men may not be motivated to chat just for the enjoyment of chatting. He's your husband, not your best girlfriend. For men, talking is work—sometimes hard work. So be careful about your expectations.

David Clarke wrote a book with the descriptive title *Men Are Clams, Women Are Crowbars*. When men clam up, many women believe it's their role in life to discover how to pry open their husbands. This can escalate into a stubborn conflict, both parties believing they're holding the moral high ground. He just wants some peace and quiet. She just wants to communicate with her husband.

So, in the interest of his need for golden silence and her need for intimate connection, I can think of no better guidance with which to close than Clarke's poignant and sage advice:

- Men: open your clams.
- Women: drop your crowbars.

TRANSLATION GUIDE

Women: His silence often means "I need some restoring quiet in order to relax and deal with stress."

Men: Her interruption of your silence means "I sometimes interpret your quietness as a rift in our relationship, and that makes me feel insecure."

1. Men, which of the ten reasons on pages 121–122 are your most common reasons for wanting silence?
2. Women, how do you frequently interpret his silence?
3. In what ways might she help her husband talk more? How might he reassure her when he needs silence?

TWENTY-FOUR

Boxes and Rubber Bands

M en like boxes.

Boxes keep life neat and structured by compartmentalizing everything into a limited number of categories. This also keeps topics and concerns separated so life doesn't get jumbled up and confusing. Everything goes into its own distinct box, and the contents of one box are never allowed to overflow into another. Men are very particular about their boxes. Each box is carefully labeled, and only what is on that label is allowed in the box. Since men are single-channeled, they dig into one box at a time and don't like to move on to the next until they've finished with and sealed up the current one.

Women like rubber bands.

Women like to connect things and hold them together. Instead of separating things, they bundle them. Since women are multi-channeled, they are not concerned with the number of things they've bundled together. Rubber bands are flexible and stretchy, always able to include one more thing. In fact, women will stretch their rubber bands to include whatever comes to mind, even if it's totally unrelated to everything else. Rubber bands have a randomness. But they hold life together.

Me? The garage is one of my boxes. It is supposed to hold tools, yard equipment, and cars. I thought I had it labeled clearly, but Tami doesn't understand the garage box. She slips things into my garage box when I'm not looking—Christmas decorations, camping gear, and all sorts of odds and ends. So I created a new box in the corner of the garage for those items so they won't contaminate my tools and equipment. But yesterday some of her stuff ended up on my workbench, mixed in with my tools. How can she do this to me?

Most women see life as a process, where everything is related to everything else. Life is a flow. To break things into rigid boxes seems unnatural and artificial. It doesn't make sense to women. Yet men see life as full of boxes. This seems logical and effective. Boxes are sturdy, dependable, predictable. They help men feel they're in control of a situation. A guy knows the rules of each box and what to expect. Men don't like changes or crises to disrupt the basic character of their boxes.

Some of the most common male boxes include:

- Work box
- Marriage box
- Finance box
- Relaxation box
- Parenting box
- Church box
- Sports box
- Romance/Sex box
- Home Maintenance box
- Relatives box

Men cling to and defend their boxes as havens of sanity.

Boxes are confusing and confining to most women. They jump from box to box (without closing any of them) or pull from three or four boxes simultaneously. They don't follow basic box etiquette. They toss things indiscriminately into the most convenient box, paying no attention to the labels. They try to merge boxes. All this can drive men crazy.

Rubber bands suit most women better than boxes. Rubber bands are pragmatic. They do whatever needs to be done, whether it feels comfortable or not. Rubber bands shrink and expand, depending on what they need to hold. Yet they are unpredictable, their load changing even minute by minute. And one can lose track of all they're keeping together or how close they are to their breaking point. Boxes rarely ever break. They might groan as they get overstuffed, but they rarely break.

Men get comfortable living in their boxes, developing unchanging patterns and routines. They like to get up at the same time, eat the same meals, and wear the same clothes. Rubber bands are constantly changing. Women like to stretch into something new or get rid of something old, to be fun and creative. To men, this tampers with our boxes. I like the way our family room looks. It's comfortable and familiar. Yet every month or so Tami likes to change something—rearrange the furniture, paint the walls, redecorate. When I first see her changes, I feel uneasy. *What did she do? The room was just great the way it was. Why did she have to change things?* But Tami is so excited about what she's done that I try to be positive and complimentary. I sit down in the room, and over time I start to get used to it. And just about the time I'm comfortable with the changes, she changes the room again.

Since a man is single-channeled, he likes to stay in one box until circumstances force him to leave. If he's at work, only the work box exists. If at home, it's the home box. If he's playing golf, it's the golf box. But as we know, women are multitaskers and rubber-band together many areas simultaneously. After all, if she doesn't deal with all these issues, who will?

Like Katie. She calls her husband, Collin, at work every once in a while to ask him a quick question or to schedule something. She learned early in their marriage to be careful about invading his work box. But sometimes she slips and starts talking about home or parenting. When this happens, Collin stops her. "Katie, can this wait until I get home?" This is his polite way of saying: *What are you doing? I'm in my work box. That's my one and only focus at this time. So don't confuse me with home stuff. I'll deal with that box when I'm there.* Katie usually gets his message and drops the subject until he gets home.

Men hate interruptions, which force them to open a second box before they're ready. Women expect interruptions. They might not like them, but they realize that interruptions are a part of life.

Men are drawn to boxes that feel comfortable and confident. They avoid as much as possible those boxes that they're not good at or aren't sure how to handle. Women rubber-band whatever they believe needs attention, regardless of their competence or knowledge of how to handle it. When stressed, men like to retreat inside the safe walls of easy boxes like sports, sex, or sleep, while pretending that the intimidating boxes don't exist. But when women are stressed, they move faster, jumping around from box to box. They also want to talk about all the jumping around and rubber-banding that must be done. Meanwhile, men are in their easy box, successfully ignoring all the other boxes. They often invite their wives to join them in their easy box. "Let's relax and watch a movie together." Or "Let's go out to dinner." But women shake their collective heads. "Look at everything that needs to be done!"

Conversations and conflicts can frequently spotlight this difference. When talking, he wants to stay on one topic or problem at a time until it's resolved. But to her, one issue reminds her of another, which brings up yet another. This also happens when he does something wrong. She brings up one mistake or failure, but before it's fully dealt with, she's dragging up additional transgressions—all rubber-banded together in her mind. All these open boxes overwhelm him to the point that he gets angry or shuts down.

Boxes and rubber bands can work together if both individuals understand and appreciate the differences. Women need to respect men's boxes. Men are going to compartmentalize life, leading to certain routines and ruts. Women must realize that this is just the way he keeps life's challenges in order so he doesn't get overwhelmed. Men, on the other hand, need to be patient with the random contents of the rubber bands. They need to step out of their boxes periodically and realize that rubber bands can be a great way of keeping things together, even though they seem messy and unfocused.

There come times in every marriage when her rubber band is the only thing holding his boxes together. And sometimes his boxes are the only way she can contain everything in her rubber band.

Together we can use our different methods to make our marriages better. For everybody needs both boxes and rubber bands.

TRANSLATION GUIDE

Men: Her mental rubber-banding of random thoughts and feelings means "Something might be neglected if I don't remember it."

Women: His mental compartmentalization means "I can't function well unless I organize life."

1. What are some of his most common boxes?
2. How do his boxes sometimes frustrate her?
3. What are some of the advantages and disadvantages of her rubber-banding everything together?

TWENTY-FIVE

The More You Give...

Tami is a giver. She's one of the most generous people I know. She gives and gives and rarely complains. She gives me cookies, compliments, cards, music, books, shirts, steak dinners, and chocolate-covered blueberries. She's even giving me the time and attention to read each of the chapters in this book. She's often busy, doing the necessities of life, or just trying to relax. But when I ask, "Could you look at this?" she generously stops what she's doing and says, "Sure." And she always gives me her thoughtful perception of what I've written, never a token offering to appease me.

Most women are natural givers in relationships. They find joy and satisfaction in giving. They love to see the smiles of appreciation. They've discovered that Jesus was right: "It is more blessed to give than to receive" (Acts 20:35). Traditionally, women are experts at providing a good meal, a clean house, an attractive appearance, a warm embrace, a strong love for their children. But, of course, they show their generosity so many other ways—giving time, energy, concern, help, prayer, forgiveness, encouragement, a listening ear, comfort, and physical gifts.

Women know how to give the right gift at the right time. And they realize that the more they give to a relationship, the better it can get.

Many women are surprised and sometimes hurt when their husbands don't share this same sense of generosity.

But the truth is that men tend naturally toward taking. They take without even thinking about it. They sometimes assume this is just the way the perfect relationship operates—she gives, he takes.

Now, let me explain that he doesn't mean to take advantage of her. He's not trying to be exploitative or take her for granted. He simply grows used to her generosity and focuses his attention on other aspects of the relationship and of life.

Women have a lot to teach men in this area. Too often we give more to our children and friends than we do to our life partners. Men need to reach out and proactively give back to their wives. A true giver...

- sees the needs and wants of others.
- spends time thinking up creative ways to give.
- gets excited about giving.
- sacrifices without a second thought.
- is liberally generous.

Unfortunately, these qualities don't come naturally to men. I want to be generous, but frequently I just don't think about it. I usually get so busy looking after my own wants and needs—or the "practical" needs of the family—that I forget about hers. When there is a crisis, I usually step up to the plate and can be incredibly generous. Also, if Tami specifically asks for something, I respond well. (Just be aware that men generally resist when they feel ordered or nagged.)

But men are not good at seeing what others need or at giving consistently, every day, for no particular reason. Generosity often doesn't cross a man's mind unless she's upset at him or someone reminds him. This is a natural blind spot. But it's also selfish, insensitive, and *stupid.*

Yes, it's stupid not to give. Because whatever a man gives to his wife, she will return to him at least twofold. A man's generosity begets her generosity. Women are often just waiting for an excuse to give more, and even a small gift will open the floodgates of her unlimited generosity. As guys, the only way we can lose is by being stingy.

At the same time, I'd encourage women to understand that their continued generosity creates the environment in which he's most likely to remember and desire to give back. And an occasional gentle reminder doesn't hurt.

But sometimes women stop giving. That's when you know something is wrong. They tend to stop when they feel hurt, unappreciated, or worn out. Husbands, pay close attention. If she's *hurt*, he needs to find out what he's done to injure her. Then hopefully he will figure out what he can do to apologize and repair the situation.

If she's feeling *unappreciated*, he needs to consider carefully all she does to make his life better. Then he can step forward to creatively, genuinely, and generously let her know how much he cherishes and values her—not only for what she gives, but for who she is. He should also be careful of negative or critical responses to her gifts; this can totally shut her down. The issue should not be the gift but appreciation for her spirit of giving.

If she's *exhausted*, he needs to come alongside her and remove some of her burden…then continue helping her, doing all he can to make her life less stressful and more rewarding.

If these three common problems for women are seriously and lovingly addressed, the giver in her will reawaken. But the longer the giving is gone, the harder it is to revive it.

When a woman stops giving, it's a sign that the relationship is out of balance. She's given so much, and he's taken so much, that she has had to retreat. Her feelings of love for her husband and hope for the relationship begin to fade. The cure is for the husband to give to his wife so generously and sacrificially, with such obvious love, that she can't possibly miss it. She must see that this isn't just a random fluke but the beginning of a new pattern of heartfelt generosity.

Now a woman's giving does have a dark side. Ninety percent of the time her giving is good. But if she turns angry, bitter, or revengeful, her giving can become hurtful. A woman's tendency to give can be twisted into a desire for payback. *He has hurt me, so I'll hurt him right back. I'll show him what it feels like.* A woman can be amazingly generous. And she can be amazingly vindictive. But vindictiveness doesn't appear without reason. It's usually the result of a deep hurt, humiliation, fear, or feeling of betrayal. There's a reason for the old saying "Hell hath no fury like a woman scorned."

Not all males lack the gift of giving. Dusty, my youngest son, has taught me a lot about generosity. When he was about six, we went out to his favorite hot dog stand. He ordered his lunch, and I paid the girl the five dollars we owed. As we walked away, Dusty asked me what the cup on the counter was all about. "It's to give the girl a tip if we want to." Dusty reached into his pocket and pulled out all the money he had (about six or seven dollars). He walked back to the stand and put it all in the cup.

"Now wait." I tried to stop him. "You gave her a bigger tip than your meal cost."

"I know," he said with a big smile.

"But that's not how you do it," I explained.

"Dad," he said softly, "she looks like she's had a hard day and needs something good."

I stood in amazement.

That day he became my hero, my example of male thoughtfulness and generosity.

CHAPTER SUMMARY

Women are natural givers, and men naturally tend to take. But even the most generous wife needs her husband to affirm and love her with gifts—even simple ones.

1. Which of you gives the most? Why? When? How?
2. What have you given each other in the past month?
3. What keeps either of you from giving more?

TWENTY-SIX

The Best Things in Life...

It was beautiful.

It was a top-of-the-line washing machine with every bell and whistle one could imagine. It was the latest designer color and had to be special-ordered. Troy was so excited to surprise his wife, Eve, with this gift. She'd been asking for a new machine for almost four years.

He worked four hours installing it himself one day while she was gone. Then the moment arrived. He led her, with her eyes closed, into the laundry room.

"Okay," he whispered. "You can look."

Her eyes fluttered open and focused on the new washer. Her impish grin fell suddenly into a look of dismay.

"This isn't what I wanted," she said.

Troy stammered in shock, "But...but look at all it can do."

"I don't care about all that fancy stuff. I showed you what I wanted."

"But this is so much bigger and better," Troy went on in growing desperation. "It can hold half again as much as the one you wanted."

"Why couldn't you just get me what I wanted?" Eve asked. Her eyes started to water. "You should know I don't care about bigger and better. I just wanted a simple washing machine."

She marched out of the room. Troy stood there confused, trying to figure out what he did wrong. *All I wanted to do was get my wife the best. What's wrong with that?*

Most men, like Troy, are competitors. The biggest catch wins the contest. A man wants to make a splash. And the bigger the splash, the more she will know he loves her. Yet that's not how most women think. In fact, they think this focus has more to do with his ego and preferences than with his love and generosity. Unfortunately, she's sometimes right. But more often it just comes down to that old translation problem between the thinking of men and women.

Size and quality are often not the highest values for a woman. She might value things like simplicity, smallness, and frugality more, along with the freedom they bring. Women sometimes feel that love gets overshadowed and lost if something is too big or too much. Since women are more detailed and subtle than men, they frequently revel in the simplicity of the small things. It's not that women can't appreciate the big things; it's just that they aren't necessary.

This is one more aspect of a woman's "language" that's hard for guys to grasp. Men think that if she likes dinner at a local café, she'll love it at an expensive restaurant. If she likes one handcrafted ornament, she'll love a set of twenty. If she likes a piece of cake, she'll love the whole cake. But women are created to love the simple things—things every guy can do. Men frequently fail to do these things because they seem too simple and too easy. Therefore, men assume the simple and easy have no value. This tragic misunderstanding leads to many missed opportunities.

Here are some simple gifts that most women love:
- a kiss on the cheek
- a card with a handwritten note
- a relaxed after-dinner conversation
- a barefoot walk on a sandy beach
- an ice-cream cone on a hot day
- a CD of love songs
- a sunset shared in silence
- an arm around her shoulder
- an attentive ear
- a genuine apology

Each one of these gifts, given with a kind and caring heart, can have a wonderful impact on a wife.

Men give less often, but when they give, they tend to go big. It's as if they're trying to make up for all the times they didn't give. The problem is that most women would rather get small gifts more often than a large gift once or twice a year. What males fail to realize is that each gift is a reminder of his love. Size or expense is not the main factor here; it's his thoughtfulness and caring. So, men, would you rather remind her weekly or only when you can afford something big? Most women would rather be reminded weekly.

Now, I'm not saying to never go big. Something big every so often can be nice and romantic. But don't use it as an excuse for not giving small things more often. Remember The Point System. If a man gives his wife a single rose twenty-four times, he has earned twenty-four points. But if he gives her two dozen roses all at once, he gets only one point (okay, maybe a point and a half).

Let me speak to the ladies for just a moment. I know that the frequency of giving is much more important to most women than the size of the gifts. But what if women were to make a little effort to translate their husbands' occasional large gifts as *expressions of large hearts*? In fact, that's often what they are. If a large gift seems worth one point, how about adding a few extra points for effort? He genuinely loves you, and in his clumsy, forgetful way, he's trying to show it to you.

At the same time, you are free to lovingly, patiently remind him of what you enjoy the most.

The truth: big isn't always the best solution. Big doesn't always fix every problem. Big doesn't always provide happiness in the long run. It might be fun and exciting at first. But if big isn't supported by the every-day small things, it soon collapses into meaninglessness.

A big house, big cars, big vacations, and even a big income left Allie feeling lonely, depressed, and broken. She sat in my office and wept. "My husband will give me anything I ever want, except himself. I live the life most women dream of, but it's empty. I'd trade it all away in a moment if I could just have his heart and time."

Many men fall into the trap of thinking, *The best way to really please her is to give her something really big.* But then if that doesn't do the job, he assumes that nothing can make her happy. And he gives up. Or he might give up because he doesn't have the time, money, or energy to do something big.

When she receives no gifts at all—little or large—she ends up feel-ing unloved, unimportant, and unappreciated. If only he knew that the genuinely loving gifts she really wants are within *any* man's reach. A compliment, a courtesy, or a cup of hot chocolate can bring a smile to her face.

In a perfect world, big gifts and small gifts are both wonderful. He learns that bigger is not necessarily better and that there is great joy in the giving of small things. Meanwhile, she learns how to celebrate the big things while reminding her husband of how much the consistent giving of the small things can truly melt her heart. Together both types of gifts enrich a marriage.

TRANSLATION GUIDE

Women: His tendency to give rarely *but big* means "I'm naturally handicapped in the giving department, but I still love you big time, and I'm showing it with a big gift."

Men: Her desire for small, *frequent* gifts means "I need to be reminded often of your love; every gift, regardless of size, says 'I love you' just as clearly."

1. Women, what do you appreciate about your husband's giving? What would you like him to do differently?
2. Men, how much do you love your wife? How do you plan to show it over the coming months?
3. When is the biggest gift the best? When is the smallest gift the best?

TWENTY-SEVEN

Strange but True

S omething was wrong.

Trudy didn't know what exactly was wrong, or why it was wrong, or even how she knew it was wrong. She didn't even know how to explain what she felt. Yet deep in her heart she knew with absolute certainty that something was definitely amiss.

When Trudy warned her husband, he tried to pinpoint her concern with a series of questions. To each of his excellent questions, she shrugged her shoulders and said, "I don't know."

"How can you not know?" he asked.

"It's just women's intuition," Trudy said with a quizzical smile.

In the end Trudy was right. She had sensed something was wrong with their twenty-year-old daughter's new roommate. She seemed nice and polite on the surface, but Trudy just knew she was hiding something.

Over the next several weeks it became apparent that this "totally honest" roommate didn't have the job she said she had. When the rent came due, she couldn't pay her portion. Soon the family also learned that the roommate was struggling with a drug habit and that her boyfriend was a dealer. Trudy had sensed the problem from the beginning, but until evidence came to light, she couldn't put her finger on the roommate's duplicity.

Everybody knows about women's intuition. Most men have seen it in their wives many times. With intuition, women sense things that are true but that can't be logically deduced from the obvious facts. It's as if they jump directly from point A to point Z without any rationale. Yet as the facts reveal themselves over time, women tend to be more right than wrong with their conclusions. It's a mysterious ability that leaves most men—and many women—baffled.

Men struggle to trust their wives' intuition. They want the tangible facts, the linear logic. If it doesn't make sense to the man, it can't be true. If he can't understand something, he questions its credibility.

Now, women frequently have the same problem. They often don't trust their own intuition because they can't defend it, explain it, or prove it. If a wife doesn't take her hunches seriously, it's hard for her husband to give them any credence.

Let me tell you about Marie. She has had two tragic marriages, in part because she ignored her intuition. Two weeks before her first wedding she wanted to cancel it, but she couldn't come up with a solid reason. She told her best friend, "It just doesn't feel right." After a long talk she dismissed her intuition as prewedding jitters. During the ceremony she didn't want to walk down the aisle. She felt physically sick, and an inner voice said, *Don't do it. This is a huge mistake.* But people talked her through it, and she got married. Over the next six months, Marie discovered that her husband was a closet alcoholic and was physically abusive. The relationship ended two years later when she caught him in bed with another woman.

Marie swore she'd never make the same mistake again. The night before her second wedding she had another strong feeling that she should cancel the ceremony. She called her father, and they talked for nearly an hour. "When you've been hurt once," he told her, "you're going to be anxious about getting hurt again. That's normal. But Dan is not the same sort of man as your first husband."

"I know, but it doesn't feel right."

"What specifically doesn't feel right?"

"I don't know." Marie groaned in frustration. "That's the problem."

"Don't go looking for trouble," her dad assured her. "Relax. I want tomorrow to be the best day of your life."

Marie stood before her second altar, and within a year she found that Dan, who looked like the perfect man on the outside, had a secret life. He consistently lied to her, had a disastrous gambling addiction, and blamed her for everything that went wrong.

"Why didn't I trust my intuition?" Marie asked as she sat in my office, tears streaming down her face.

Women have amazing intuitions. If a red flag pops up in a woman's mind, it almost always proves to be true.

Women operate within the realm of feelings and instincts. Men, on the other hand, operate within the realm of facts and principles. Men have *insight*, based on clear-cut, rational, observable facts. If they don't have the facts, they question the concern. Men like to problem-solve and fix things; if they don't have all the facts, it's hard for them to do this. Insight is logical, analytical, objective. It tends to be black-and-white, while intuition tends to be fuzzy. That is why most men don't know what to do with intuition. It's not clear-cut and linear. It doesn't obey their rules of logic. If men don't know what to do with something, they ignore it, minimize it, or reject it.

In the case of intuition, that is a big mistake.

Men tend to be more drawn to mechanical, mathematical, and scientific fields. Women like emotions and relationships, which are frequently messy and unpredictable. They are intuitive areas. But they are *not* illogical; they simply operate on a relational logic, which is more complex and speculative than linear logic.

Insight helps people organize the facts, but intuition helps people read between the facts and at times extrapolate beyond the facts. Both are valuable, for insight and intuition, working in tandem, can be a great team.

As a husband learns to accept and appreciate his wife's intuition, he'll discover at least six areas in which she can provide invaluable perspective:

1. *Your children.* A mother has a unique bond with her children, and she may see problems with attitude, judgment, emotions, choices, or friends before the father sees them.

2. *Other women.* A wife has the ability to sense when another woman has a hidden agenda, a deceptive spirit, or a romantic interest in her husband, no matter how subtle.

3. *Your honesty.* A wife can tell when her husband is being anything less than totally honest.

4. *Your emotions.* A wife can often recognize and read her husband's emotions faster and more effectively than he can.

5. *People in general.* A woman can frequently sense whether someone is safe, honest, or trustworthy by spending a few minutes with them, even if she's never met the person before.

6. *Your relationship.* A wife has an amazing ability to sense how her marriage is doing—whether it's healthy or not and what areas need the most attention.

In each of these situations a woman might not be able to identify exactly what's wrong or why it's wrong, but when she senses trouble, it's almost always somewhere near.

Intuition isn't flawless. Women must be careful to not allow their fears or insecurities to skew their intuition. Exaggeration or distortion might easily take a legitimate concern and turn it into a major crisis. On the other hand, men must be careful not to minimize intuition simply because it has no easily explainable factual base. I've learned that the balance point between these concerns is to always take a woman's intuition seriously. But don't panic. Assume that the intuition has validity while actively looking for facts to substantiate it.

Earlier today an eighty-five-year-old lady said it as directly as anyone I've ever heard: "My thoughts and emotions have gotten confused many times in my long life, but I've learned that my intuition doesn't lie to me."

TRANSLATION GUIDE

Men: You need to trust your wife's intuition because it's more often right than wrong, even if she can't prove it.

Women: You need to respect your husband's insight; he can identify evidence either to support your intuition or to show that your emotions might be misleading you.

1. Describe three situations when her intuition proved right.
2. In which of the six areas on page 143 does she have the best intuition? Give some examples.
3. Describe three times his insight has been accurate and helpful.

TWENTY-EIGHT

The Securities Trade

Why don't you love me?" Robyn rested both fists on her hips, elbows out.

"I love you," Ryan protested. "What would make you think I don't?"

"Everything." Her defiance dissolved into tears.

Ryan stared at her. *How am I supposed to respond to that? If she doesn't know I love her by now, I give up.* In confusion and frustration he left the room to ponder the problem.

As soon as he was gone, she cried even harder. "Why would he just walk out on me? He really must not love me."

What we have here is just one more translation problem. Ryan loves Robyn, but she doesn't feel it. The ways in which he shows his love don't work for her. His methods may be nice, but they don't touch her heart. Women need to *feel* loved. This usually means a woman feels:

1. *Prioritized.* She feels she's the most important person or thing in his life. He shows this to her through his everyday actions and attitudes.

2. *Prized.* She feels she's treasured and valued by him. He verbalizes this to her and to others regularly.

3. *Protected.* She feels she's defended from danger. He will do all he can to ensure her safety, comfort, and security.

A woman yearns to be loved by her husband, and one of her greatest fears is that he might someday fall out of love with her. When she fears the loss of love, whether her fear is valid or not, she begins to slip into insecurity. At times her mind races nonstop: *What if he finds somebody younger, prettier, thinner, smarter, nicer, more athletic, more generous, more organized, less emotional, less stubborn, lower-maintenance...*

Men might experience financial or occupational insecurity but rarely relational insecurity. In fact, they tend to take their wives' love for granted. Love is important to men, but it's not their top relationship need. What they yearn for most is to be respected. Men need their wives to believe the best about them. To be disrespected by his wife can be devastating to a man. At best it's an emotional injury; at worst it's a humiliating blow, a betrayal that can build a wall of anger, mistrust, and withdrawal.

A man flourishes when respected. Most importantly, he needs respect with regard to his...

- opinions
- words
- abilities
- motives
- reputation
- work
- intentions
- character
- accomplishments

To not respect these aspects of her husband is to not respect him at all. At least that's how it feels to him.

Women fear loss of love; men fear loss of respect. The apostle Paul wrote about this when he insisted that "each one of you also must love his wife as he loves himself, and the wife must respect her husband" (Ephesians 5:33).

Men are often shocked and baffled that their wives would ever question their love. Yet women need to know that their husbands' love is solid and consistent and ever present. To most women, secure love means some, if not all, of the following:

1. He still communicates his love for her.
2. He's committed to the marriage.
3. He's not consistently upset with or angry at her.
4. He's not tempted elsewhere.
5. He's going to be there for her.
6. He provides for her.
7. He listens to her.
8. He's concerned about her needs.
9. He gives her quality time.
10. He holds her when she's scared.
11. He's patient with her.
12. He's a safe person who won't hurt her.

A husband believes that his wife should trust his love, even if he doesn't meet any of the above criteria. Yet a wife needs to *see* and *feel* his love in order to trust it.

To most men, love without respect is meaningless sentimentality. If he doesn't feel respected, he may initially respond with anger or defensiveness. If it continues, he will sooner or later emotionally or physically withdraw. This can create a situation where another woman, who shows him more respect, can steal away his heart. Just as women tend to be more sensitive to insecurity, men tend to be more sensitive to shame. Most men would rather die than be shamed. Shame steals his masculinity, leaving him embarrassed and humiliated. It strips him of all he believes he should be. Some men may appear to handle shame without reacting, but I guarantee you that is only outward appearance. On the inside he is cringing.

If most women really understood what disrespect does to a man, they'd stop immediately. At least, I hope they would.

Allison didn't understand. And she relentlessly refused to stop.

Christopher was forgetful. He knew this was a problem, so he tried to write everything down. But sometimes even that didn't help. One evening he was to meet Allison, his wife, for dinner at an expensive restaurant with several other couples. It was a cold night, so Allison had asked Chris to bring her coat. He forgot. Allison was angry, and she let him know it in front of their dinner partners. He knew he deserved her anger, but what he got was crushing wrath.

Allison accused him of being selfish and insensitive. She looked him in the eye and said, "What's wrong with you? Are you stupid? Can't you do anything right? What kind of a husband can't even take care of his wife? I don't know why I put up with you." All the tables around them could hear her words, dripping with contempt and sarcasm. Chris felt ill. Over and over he tried to apologize, but she replied, "I'm sick of your worthless little apologies. If you could do it right the first time, you wouldn't have to apologize."

Allison broke every rule about respecting one's husband. She embarrassed and humiliated him. She criticized him. She belittled him. She showed contempt for him. She attacked his person and masculinity. She trapped him in a corner and gave him no way out. And on top of all this, she did it in public. Why didn't she just put a gun to his head and pull the trigger?

Chris sat in my office and said, "I love my wife, but she's killing it. I can't take much more of this. If she can't show me any respect, this relationship is over."

Every man needs his wife to show him respect in at least three powerful ways:

1. *Forgiveness.* Let go of his mistakes; don't bring them up or even think about them. As Gary Rosberg wrote, "Show grace with his failures."
2. *Encouragement.* Find creative ways to build him up by focusing on his positives. To discourage him with words, tone of voice, or attitude is dangerous.
3. *Appreciation.* Compliment him every day, letting him know how grateful you are for all the big and little things he does to make your life easier and more fulfilling.

If every woman would regularly ask herself, *Does my husband feel respected by me?* and *Have I done anything today that might feel disrespectful to him?* she would grow more sensitive to this all-important male need. Likewise, if every man would ask himself, *Does my wife feel completely loved by me?* and *Have I done anything today that might feel uncaring or unloving to her?* he would become more attentive to her tender heart.

What's more, each amplifies the other in reciprocal fashion. The more a man loves his wife, the more she'll show respect to him. And the more a woman respects her husband, the more he'll show love to her. It's a chicken-and-egg kind of arrangement. But don't worry about which should have come first. If you're a chicken, lay an egg. If you're an egg, hatch a chicken. Faithfully do your part, and watch your relationship grow.

TRANSLATION GUIDE

Men: Her need to feel loved means "I feel abandoned and insecure unless I'm regularly reassured of your love for me, and I can't help this."

Women: His need to feel respected means "I can crumble inside, in shame and lost confidence, when you disrespect me."

1. How does he show his love for her? Give examples of the three principles on pages 146–147.
2. How does she show her respect for him? Give examples of the three principles on page 150.
3. When is it hardest for you to show love or respect? Why?

TWENTY-NINE

Power Plays

Women nag when they're desperate.

"Then my wife sure must be desperate," said Roy. "Suzie nags me morning, noon, and night. But it doesn't do any good."

"Why not?" I asked.

"Oh, I just tune it out."

"But don't you get tired of it?"

"Sure I do. But I'm not giving in. I'm not letting her control me. All nagging does is get me angry. The more she nags, the angrier I get. And then I'm not going to do anything she wants."

"Sounds like you get pretty stubborn."

"Stubborn or not"—Roy pounded his knee with his fist—"I'm not letting anyone boss me around."

Women call it reminding, asking, or insisting. One woman calls it "compulsive encouragement." But whatever they call it, most men see it as nagging. Men almost universally hate nagging. They see it as controlling, pushy, and often demeaning. Yet this usually isn't what a woman intends. Women don't want to be nags and frequently don't even realize when they've slipped into the role. But any time someone makes a request more than three times in a twenty-four-hour period, it's nagging.

A woman nags because she doesn't know what else to do. Maybe…

1. *She feels he's not listening.* If she says something emphatically over and over, maybe he'll hear her request and do it.

2. *She doesn't think he understands.* If she repeats it enough different ways, maybe he'll grasp how important the request is to her.

3. *She's not sure how else to motivate him.* If she provides steady pressure over a long period, maybe he'll develop a desire to do it.

4. *She's hurt that he doesn't act.* If she vents how hurt, disappointed, or angry she is about his inaction, maybe he'll follow through out of remorse.

Nagging, for whatever reason, is basically saying, "I want you to do something." A man's lack of response often means, "I'll do it when I'm good and ready, so give me some space."

Men hear nagging as a push for power, an attack on their autonomy and independence, and ultimately a threat to their masculinity. In the language of men, they interpret nagging as manipulation that forces them into a one-down or subservient position. Therefore men become passive-aggressively resistant to anything that remotely resembles nagging.

A common scenario goes like this: a wife tells her husband something she wants (or needs) him to do. It may be a simple request, but if he responds immediately, to him it's like bowing to her control. So he waits a while before doing it. That way when he does respond to her request, it looks as if he's doing it of his own free will. Now, in a woman's language, she can't understand his being resistant, so she assumes maybe he's forgotten her request. Impatiently, she repeats it. Which now means he has to put off the task once again, until he feels that he's not doing it because of her pressure. The danger is that he frequently waits so long that he genuinely does forget. He doesn't mean to disregard her request, but that is, in fact, what he does. Each time she asks, he puts it off longer so he won't appear to be a henpecked husband.

In the end she demands, "Why won't you do anything I ask?"

To which he replies, "I'd do it if you'd just stop nagging."

"I'm not nagging," she insists.

As emotions intensify, both feel controlled, unappreciated, and disconnected. But let's be honest: sometimes women nag, and sometimes men get stubborn. Both partners need to lighten up. A man needs to realize that his wife might resort to nagging as her last-ditch attempt to capture his attention. She feels ignored and yearns desperately for a connection—any type of connection—even if it's by creating a crisis. If she can't get a positive connection, she'll settle for a negative one. Most women will do almost anything to feel closer.

At this point many wives ask, "So if I can't nag, what can I do? What will get through to him?" Here are a few ideas:

- Send him an e-mail.
- Write your request on his bathroom mirror in lipstick.
- Always say please.
- Don't demand.
- Be patient.
- Beware of using guilt or manipulation.
- Watch your tone of voice.
- Accept the fact that things don't always go the way you wish.

In the restaurant industry they say, "Presentation is everything." Approach him with words like, "When you get a chance, would you please help me?" or, "I really appreciate it when you do this. When you get the time, would you mind doing it again?" Then give him at least a half hour. If you have to repeat yourself, say something like, "I'm not pushing. I was just wondering when you thought you could get to it." If he doesn't follow through with your request, let it go. Your world won't collapse. If he does follow through, let him know how appreciative you are.

And men need to remember that women wouldn't nag if we responded more quickly. A prompt, generous response isn't a sign of weakness.

It's a sign of love.

TRANSLATION GUIDE

Women: His delay in fulfilling your requests means "I want to please you, but submitting to nagging wounds my masculinity."

Men: Her nagging means "You seem either stubborn or forgetful, and I'm getting desperate to know that you take me seriously."

1. How often does she nag? Why does she nag?
2. How does he respond to her nagging?
3. What are better ways than nagging to get his attention and assure his follow-through?

THIRTY

The Buck—Stop It or Pass It?

Emily observed Duncan's fuming until she couldn't stand it any longer. "Why are you mad at me?"

"I'm not mad at you," he answered. "I'm just frustrated with work. Nothing has gone right on this project."

"But every time you talk to me, you have this irritated tone of voice. You sure act like I've done something wrong. Are you positive you aren't upset at me?"

"Emily," Duncan said firmly, "I'm absolutely positive. Work is driving me nuts. My frustration has nothing to do with you."

"There's that tone of voice again." Emily suddenly looked worried. "I know I haven't been a perfect wife and things have been a little hectic around the house lately. But I promise next week will be a lot better."

A lot of women are like Emily—they're blame magnets. They personalize problems. If something is wrong, they often think it must be their fault. If they had been faster, smarter, kinder, more careful, more talented, or whatever, certain problems wouldn't have happened. Women beat themselves up far too much. They worry, overanalyze, and ruminate over any potential flaw or mistake until they make themselves sick. They wonder what they have done wrong and what they should have done better. If everything isn't perfect, they feel like they must have let people down. Women share their successes with others, taking less credit than they deserve. Yet they shoulder failures alone, even when those failures are not theirs.

A lot of men are blame repellers. They react defensively toward problems. They tend to come up with all sorts of reasons why something is not their fault. They minimize or explain away their responsibility when things go wrong. While women internalize problems, men externalize them. Men point outward to explain what went awry. They proclaim: "It's not my fault." Then they find something or someone to blame—the government, the weather, the job, the children, the world. There are hundreds of things to blame. Men have a hard time seeing their part in what has gone wrong and then taking responsibility for it. This is one reason men don't apologize. If a person doesn't think he's done anything wrong, why apologize?

It's interesting how men and women can see situations so differently.

He says	She says
"The test questions were too hard."	"I didn't study hard enough."
"They slammed on their brakes too fast."	"I was following too close."
"The boss didn't give me a fair chance."	"I should have pushed harder."
"What's wrong with the kids?"	"What's wrong with me as a parent?"

As with so many things in life, the balance is somewhere in the middle. Sometimes a person should take personal responsibility. And sometimes the blame really does lie elsewhere. Many situations involve a combination of the two—the blame should be shared.

Women tend to look for what they might have done wrong and then get upset about it. This drives their husbands crazy. A man might be frustrated by work, finances, friends, children, church, traffic, or life in general. His wife intuits his frustration and assumes it's her fault. *I must have offended him. He must be upset with me. What have I done this time?* And he has the hardest time convincing her that his attitude has nothing to do with her.

I frequently encourage wives to stop making assumptions and simply ask, "Are you upset with me, or is it something else?" Most of the time it's something else. When he says so, she needs to relax and believe him. If indeed she's upsetting him, he will tell her. Guys have no problem blaming others, especially their wives.

So, women, be careful about personalizing and taking too much responsibility. This leads to two potential dangers:

1. *Perfectionism.* You'll never do everything perfectly, and that's okay. Sometimes bad things just happen. Sure, you might have been able to anticipate a problem and do something amazing to stop it, but you're only human.

2. *Codependency.* You're not responsible for his feelings, thoughts, or behaviors—even if he tries to blame you. No wife can stop or change her husband unless that's something he truly wants and is willing to work for.

Personalizing takes responsibility for too much and increases a woman's anxiety, leaving her worn out and discontented. She often feels that she can't fully relax, because if she does, something will fall apart.

Men need to be careful about their defensiveness and blaming; they also risk two potential dangers:

1. *Emotional distance.* Constant defensiveness builds a wall between the two of you. Admitting fault shows vulnerability, drawing your wife closer and allowing her to see your imperfections. Then she may even love you more.

2. *Irresponsibility.* Some things are just your fault. Blaming often appears immature and irresponsible, especially if it's unfairly directed toward your wife. Remember, she's probably already beating herself up; she doesn't need your help.

Defensiveness usually doesn't take enough responsibility; it isolates a man and blocks his relationship from growing. His self-protectiveness gives him the illusion of being in control and in a one-up position. But it pushes her into a one-down position, which either reduces her self-esteem or increases her frustration at him for not taking responsibility.

Let's eavesdrop on Emily and Duncan after they've had a chance to figure out some of these principles.

Emily notices Duncan sitting silently on the front porch swing, a frown on his face. "Are you upset at me?" she asks.

"No, I'm just thinking."

"Are you sure?" she prods.

"I said I was just thinking," he snaps back. "Why does everything have to be a problem? Can't you just believe me for once and give me some space?"

"Okay," Emily says gently. "I know I worry too much and take things personally. But I love you so much that I don't want to do anything to upset you."

"I'm sorry I got short with you." Duncan's voice and face soften. "Sometimes I need a little space to clear my head, and I don't want you always thinking something's wrong. I love you even if I'm brooding alone."

"Thanks for the reassurance. I needed to know everything's okay with us."

At times, every husband and wife overreact to each other. It happens whenever two people live in close proximity for very long. She worries and personalizes. He defends and blames. She gets hurt. He gets angry.

Why do things get out of control? The answer is simple: he's acting like a man, and she's acting like a woman.

Let's learn to relax. Don't assume it's the end of the world. Reassure each other of your love and commitment. Give each other a kiss. And move on.

Life is too short to waste.

TRANSLATION GUIDE

Men: Her self-blaming means "I take problems—especially your unhappiness—personally and think I've done something wrong."

Women: His defensiveness means "I fear being wrong, so I defend my ego with excuses and blame-casting."

1. How often does she personalize, and how does he respond to it?
2. How often does he get defensive, and how does she respond to it?
3. Does her personalizing lead to perfectionism or codependency? Does his defensiveness lead to emotional distance or irresponsibility?

THIRTY-ONE

Track Stars and Volleyball Players

Track is a loner's sport. Each contestant competes on his own. (Okay, I'm ignoring relay races. But bear with me.) He depends only on himself, so he has no one else to let him down and no one else to interfere with his strategy. He's independent.

Volleyball is a sport for the gregarious. Teammates talk to one another and depend on one another. They practice for hours and weeks outside of their matches and work up team strategies. They're interdependent.

Men are track stars. Women are volleyball players. But in marriage they're forced to play a strange new hybrid—a game we'll call *trolleyball*. This game forces an independent track star to share life with an interdependent volleyball player. A lot of couples have trouble playing trolleyball. They can't agree on the rules.

Take Bob and Cindi. Bob could barely contain his excitement as he snuck up behind Cindi in the kitchen.

"Ta-da!" He jumped in front of her, flourishing a colorful brochure.

"What's this?" Cindi chuckled at his antics, then tried to read the brochure in his waving hand.

"It's about Camp Get-ridda-kidda." Bob acted like he was about to wet his pants. "I just signed the twins up for camp!"

"What?" Cindi was suddenly flabbergasted—but not in a good way. "What have you done?"

"Well, you keep telling me we need some alone time. I just bought us a whole week." He swallowed hard, trying to endure her glare. "You even said you'd heard this was a great camp."

Cindi snatched the brochure away from Bob and opened it. But before she could read it, she threw it back at him. "I can't believe you did this without even talking to me." She stormed off into their bedroom and slammed the door.

Bob picked up the crumpled brochure off the floor, muttering, "I guess I can't do anything right."

What went wrong? Bob thought he had run a record hundred-yard dash; he'd tried to do something good. But Cindi expected him to set the ball for her spike; he had left her out of the process.

Men like to make decisions independently, while women like to make decisions together. Men like to just go out and do something, while women like to interact, explore, and communicate. By interacting about issues, most women feel closer and more connected.

To most men, independent decision making is a strength. It shows confidence and leadership—part of being a husband and father. But most women see independent decision making as selfish and inconsiderate. The exceptions include areas that are, by common agreement, strictly "his" job or "her" job. They also include areas for which she has acknowledged she has no interest, no competency, or no time. Otherwise, women don't want to be left out or pushed away; they want to be listened to and taken seriously. When men's independent decisions affect their wives, women feel disregarded and marginalized.

Yet most guys tell themselves: *Why should I have to talk about this? I shouldn't have to explain myself all the time.* Collaborating feels like asking permission, which seems belittling to them. They think the issue through, consider the options, weigh the pros and cons, make their decision, and announce it to their wives. It's a done deal.

A man says at this point, "Trust me."

His wife says, "It's not an issue of trust, but of working together, caring for each other, showing mutual respect. And most of all it's an issue of love. If you really loved me, you'd include me in big decisions."

When he hears this line of thinking, he scratches his head. "What in the world does love have to do with decision making?"

Women want to discuss, negotiate, ask questions, relate feelings, and consider compromises. They see collaboration as an opportunity to draw closer. Men see it as an unnecessary complication—a slow, clumsy, ineffective method. They could deal with the issue so much more quickly, cross it off their list, and move on with life. Independence seems neat, while interdependence can be messy. And dangerous—all those emotions.

Men like action and movement. So they fixate on the decision. But women's central concern is: *how will this affect our relationship?* Action and movement are irrelevant, and they'll defer decision making indefinitely if that's what it takes to find common ground. In order to work toward the best decision, women might also reach out to friends, family, books, or counselors. All of this drives many men crazy; it feels like a slap in the face that tells them they're incompetent. This drives them to want to be even more independent, to prove they can make a decision on their own. Besides, the man strongly believes everything will work out fine and she will ultimately accept whatever decision he makes. But even if she *does* like his decision, she still may be disappointed that she was not part of the process.

As when my parents decided to have a moving sale. Dad started pulling out stuff that they no longer needed or hadn't used in years. Mom was encouraged and appreciative of all his hard work. That is, until she discovered he'd sold her record collection from college. To him this was a no-brainer. Many of the records were scratched, and they no longer even had a turntable to play them. But Mom was hurt and angry.

"How could you sell my records?" she asked.

"You hadn't listened to them in thirty years."

"But they were mine. Why didn't you even ask me?"

"Well, somebody had to make a decision, and you were busy."

Dad had tried to be helpful, but his independence had been hurtful. I asked Dad why he hadn't consulted Mom about selling her records. He stared at me, perplexed, and said, "I didn't think I needed to."

Most men don't think about their independence. It's just the way they are. *Why ask about it? Why talk about it? I can handle the situation myself.* Every man has a little general inside who wants to charge forward. He doesn't want to falter or appear unsure. Even little boys like to direct and command, whereas little girls like to request and suggest. Men want to point out the way to go and have their wives just follow their lead; women want to understand the whys, hows, and whens.

If only men would understand that interdependence is actually a positive thing. It can improve their relationships and bring them closer to their wives. Men are risk takers, but this can threaten their wives' security. As a husband and wife talk about potentially risky decisions, she becomes more willing to risk, and he softens the risk factors as he becomes more sensitive to her concerns. That's how they both win.

Likewise, if a woman wouldn't take his independence so personally, she might respond with greater understanding of his heart. Men are often independent without even thinking about it. They don't mean to be insensitive or leave their wives out. Men are simply marching forward like good buffaloes. They are, for this moment, living in their decision box, not in their relationship box.

Every relationship needs a healthy balance. Let the husband have points of independence. And let the wife have points of interdependence. That way she learns to respect his ownership of certain decisions in which she need have no input. And he comes to appreciate the wisdom of interacting over certain decisions even if it slows down and muddies the process.

Sometimes he needs to feel the confident independence of a good sprint. And sometimes she needs his teamwork to set up the killer spike.

Besides, who said marriage was always going to go your way?

TRANSLATION GUIDE

Women: His independent decision making means "Let's get the job done quickly and cleanly; that way we can get more done."

Men: Her desire for interdependence means "Interacting over a decision strengthens our relationship, and that's as important to me as making the decision."

1. In what ways does he tend to act independently?
2. How does she respond to his independence?
3. In what areas is interdependence most important to both of you?

THIRTY-TWO

Friends in Deed

S tella was so glad for Clay's day off. She veritably bounced with anticipation. "Let's talk," she said.

After a long pause, Clay asked, "What do you want to talk about?"

"I don't care. Whatever you want to talk about."

Clay sat perplexed. He didn't want to talk about anything. But he
was smart enough to know that if he said so, she'd be offended. She'd
think he didn't care. He enjoyed being with his wife, but he didn't need
to talk all the time to feel close. This whole talking thing was her idea,
so why was it suddenly up to him to think of a topic?

For most women, talk is the glue that holds a relationship together. It
tells her:

- She's not alone.
- She's important.
- She's taken seriously.
- She's truly loved.
- She's part of a team.
- She's close to and connected with her husband.

Talk provides a sense of security and well-being to most women. They feel, *If we can talk, everything is okay.* Talk is frequently the key to her heart.

Yet when a woman says to her husband, "We need to talk," cold chills run down his back. *Oh no, what's wrong? What have I done this time? She must be upset about something.* Men don't need talk to achieve security. In fact, to many men, talking things out holds the risk of making things worse. Remember, he likes the simplicity and cleanness of the solo race to the finish line. And after a problem is solved, when she wants to debrief in detail (more talk!), he waves his hand and says, "Just let it be."

Men tend to believe that what you do is more important than what you say. As one man told me, "Anybody can say anything. Why should I trust somebody's words? People lie all the time. Or maybe they just say what they think you want to hear. But if you actually *do* something kind or positive, then a person knows you really care." For men, words can be false or manipulative or meaningless—just words. It's action that shows where one's heart really is.

Since women use words to build closeness, even if there is nothing to talk about, they will make small talk—weather, fashions, gossip, or whatever. Most men suck at small talk. To them, if you don't have something important to say, don't say anything at all.

Women cement their especially close connections by listening to and telling secrets. In fact, whom a woman trusts with her secrets determines who her best friends are. Men don't tell secrets; that might make them appear weak or vulnerable. And they don't like to hear secrets; that feels as if they're violating someone's privacy—even their wives'. The more personal a conversation, the more disengaged most men will appear. In many situations, talking doesn't cause a man to feel close—it simply makes him uncomfortable.

Women often see the right words as the potential cure-all to any relationship problem. To them, most relationship problems are really communication problems. But men often think that *cutting down* on communication is the best way to improve it.

Men are physical. They like to jump in and do things. They like to be active in a hands-on sort of way. When children play, the boys tend to be more energetic and animated. They run, jump, climb, and wrestle. Even as adults, when guys play cards, they get into the game. A conversation is fine as long as it doesn't interfere with the game. When women play cards, the game is only an excuse to socialize. For men, it's the *experience* that's meaningful in and of itself. Talk distracts them from the enjoyment of the activity. But that's not a problem for some men, who've learned how to tune out the talk so they can more effectively focus on the moment.

Men like to keep busy, whether it's working hard on a project or relaxing in front of the television. Yet since men are not multi-taskers, they have a hard time working *or* relaxing if someone is talking.

Whereas women share verbal expressions, men share experiences, preferably in silence. A man can enjoy simply hanging out with his wife in the same room. He's happy just knowing she's there, even if they never exchange a word. He might watch her for a moment or two, or he may touch her shoulder or back as he passes by. He enjoys a wonderful sense of connection and well-being in this silence, which most women don't understand. A little talk may be acceptable, but too much talk can ruin the atmosphere. To most men, this physical closeness is much more powerful and affirming than verbal closeness. In fact, to many men, *verbal* and *closeness* are two words that just don't fit together.

Women enjoy communication that is focused. This allows them to fully enjoy its relational and emotional content. But eye contact and full attention often make men so uncomfortable and self-conscious that they shut down. They may communicate best when half their attention can be focused elsewhere. If a woman wants her husband to talk more, she might converse while driving, walking, playing a game, or working side by side. He is most likely to be verbal when he's doing something physical—but not something that requires his undistracted attention. That's when talk gets in the way.

We all like to stay within our safety zones. Women feel safe and comfortable with verbal interaction. Men feel best with physical activities. Silence is safe for most men. They remember all the times they have said foolish, insensitive, or hurtful things without meaning to. So they remind themselves, *Keep your mouth shut and you won't get into trouble.* Silence becomes their default protective mode. Granted, it can also be used as a punishment or power mode, but it's more likely they simply want to avoid trouble or misunderstanding. Most men fall back to the simple questions: Why talk? What's the purpose? What will it accomplish?

I just invited Tami to read over this chapter. When she had finished, she shook her head.

"What's wrong with what I've said?" I asked.

"Nothing," she said, still shaking her head. "I just can't understand why men and women are so different."

That old translation problem again.

When another woman read this she said, "Well, this will give my husband and me a lot to talk about."

To that husband, wherever you are, I'm sorry!

TRANSLATION GUIDE

Men: Her need to talk means "Words equal love to me."

Women: His reluctance to talk means "I often trust action more than words."

1. Why are words so important to her? Why aren't they as important to him?
2. Women, which of the six messages of meaningful conversation on page 168 are most important to you?
3. Men, what kinds of action or shared experience speak love and comfort to you?

THIRTY-THREE

The Ins and Outs of Emotions

Everything seemed to be going so well. That's what puzzled Nathan. "Why are you crying?" he asked his wife, Molly.

"Because I'm so happy." Molly cried even harder.

Nathan blinked. "You cry when you're happy? This doesn't make any sense. Last time you cried, your feelings were hurt."

Molly laughed through her tears. "I cry for a lot of reasons. I also cry when I'm angry or embarrassed or tired. Sometimes I cry when I'm confused and don't know *what* I feel."

"But if *you* don't know what you feel, how in the world can *I* ever figure it out?"

"You don't have to." Molly put her arms around her husband. "Just accept me and love me, even if I don't make any sense."

Women tend to be more open with their emotions. It's accepted and expected. That's just the way it is. Men have strong emotions; they just aren't as expressive with them. Men deny and stuff their emotions as much as possible, especially if the feelings are related to grief, hurt, or embarrassment. Women tend to spotlight their feelings by talking them out with friends or family. Men tend to work their feelings out physically, most often alone. When men start to get emotional, they try to override the feelings. Or they look for something to do to distract them. They get busy. They get physical.

When hard emotions move close, I want to get outside and walk. Some guys need to exercise, chop wood, shoot baskets, ride their bikes, attack a project—anything that gives them physical exertion and space. Men frequently don't feel comfortable with their own emotions, let alone hers. Men aren't sure how to explore or express their feelings. And even if they know how, why would they want to?

While women are more emotional, men tend to be more visual. What they see captures their attention and pulls them in. This is why advertisers use physically attractive and sexually provocative women to promote cars, beer, and everything in between. After a hard day's work, many men are visually drawn to the television. Here they can sit down, relax, and become absorbed in what they see. Men like to watch action and activity—almost any kind. They will watch television for hours, even stupid or worthless programming. It's something to watch. They'll also watch people and cars and the changing weather. When they go fishing, they'll sit all day and simply watch the river go by.

Here are a few of the contrasts between men's visualness and women's emotionality.

Men	Women
Easily visually distracted	Easily emotionally impacted
Deeper visual absorption	Deeper emotional sensitivities
Stronger visual memory	Stronger emotional memory
Visual mode triggers emotional reaction	Emotional reactions shape relationships
Visuals are directly linked to physical arousal	Emotions are linked to physical arousal

These five parallel truths can draw a couple closer, or they can pull a relationship far apart.

Because of these differences, smart women give their husbands something attractive to look at. And smart men give their wives positive emotional connections. Men are more drawn to their wives when they take care of their physical appearance. I know this sounds shallow to many women. But this is part of men's built-in visual orientation. Men can't ignore what they see. (I should acknowledge that a man's appearance is important to his wife also, but usually more for emotional reasons.)

Now, if a wife has let herself go physically, this is not an excuse for a husband to act unlovingly. It just means he needs to be more patient with her. On the other hand, a wife needs to understand that her appearance can create a visual block, which may distress or distract her husband from giving her all the love she deserves. In a weight-conscious, appearance-oriented culture, this is the last thing most women want to hear. But unfortunately it's something that is important to most men.

To help meet a man's visual needs, a wife can make reasonable efforts to look her best. Attractiveness has to do with things like weight, clothing, makeup, and hairstyle. But it also has a lot to do with attitude. A woman of average attractiveness can look radiant when a loving, positive attitude shines through. Inner beauty can elevate a woman's physical appearance significantly. Dr. Willard Harley writes, "Attractiveness is what you do with what you have."

But let's be honest. As a woman gets older, appearances change. It's harder to lose weight; one's complexion isn't as clear; things begin to sag and stretch. Life is hard on a body. Because of this reality, men must be realistic in their expectations. When a man becomes obsessed or demanding of a certain level of physical perfection, he hurts his wife and triggers her insecurity. She then starts to believe that if she isn't at her very best, he might not love her.

When it comes to appearance, guys are lucky. Yes, women want their husbands to look their best, but this is secondary to other qualities such as kindness, character, and connectedness.

To men, connectedness starts with what they see. To women, connectedness starts with how they feel.

When a husband takes care of his wife emotionally, she will be motivated to look her best. Complimenting her appearance while minimizing her imperfections will bolster her self-confidence and cause her to draw closer to him. Just as women need to be there visually for their men, so men need to be there emotionally for their wives. Men need to relax, giving themselves permission to let out their feelings. A man can be strong and still express what's in his heart. This sort of vulnerability makes him more attractive to his wife. And what adds to this attractiveness is his ability to embrace *her* emotions. How might he do this?

1. *Acknowledge* what she's feeling and any situation that might have evoked the feelings.
2. *Ask* her about her emotions, and encourage her to talk about them.
3. *Affirm* her right to feel whatever she might be feeling, without apology.
4. *Accept* her emotions as valid, even if they seem irrational or confusing to you.
5. *Appreciate* her emotional depth and ability to express what's on her heart.
6. *Apologize* if you have been responsible for any of her negative emotions.
7. *Approach* her with compassion and support as you help her deal with difficult feelings.

As men are willing to be more emotionally approachable and sensitive to their wives, they might be surprised at the positive dividends they receive.

Samantha, on the other hand, seemed to have nothing left to give back to her husband. Her reservoirs were depleted, and she looked depressed. She had lost the sparkle in her eye and the vivaciousness of her step.

I was concerned. "What's happened?" I asked.

"I can't do anything right," she said. "My husband is constantly complaining about my looks, my attitude, my cooking, my organization skills. When I try to tell him how this makes me feel, he says I'm overreacting. It's no use. I might as well just keep my mouth shut."

"But look what it's done to you," I said.

"I can't help it," she said with a lethargy that broke my heart.

As I sat beside Samantha and tried to encourage her, all I could think was how tragic and unnecessary this situation was. Because Samantha's husband didn't connect with her emotionally, she had lost the desire to connect with him visually. And because she didn't connect with him visually, he had pushed her away emotionally. In the end they both lost.

You, however, can turn this downward spiral on its head and let your relationship soar.

Just as one type of neglect feeds the other, so one spouse's caring attention will enable and amplify the other's.

At times you might find yourselves so happy that you'll *both* cry.

TRANSLATION GUIDE

Men: Your wife needs you to care for her emotionally.

Women: Your husband needs you to care for him visually.

1. In what ways and in what situations does he express his emotions?
2. How can she attend more to her appearance in ways that might please him?
3. Which of the seven ways on page 176 are best for him to connect with her emotionally?

THIRTY-FOUR

Playing with Fire

"When did it start?" I asked.

"At thirteen I looked at porn for the first time," said Trevor. He stared at the pancakes he'd just ordered. The restaurant was noisy enough that he could speak candidly without the fear of being overheard. "It was at my best friend's house. His father had a stack of magazines and a few dirty movies hidden in the back of his garage. The more I looked, the more I wanted."

"Did things change when you got married?"

"During the first few months everything was great, but then I went to a strip club with some old buddies. When Julie asked why I was out so late, I lied to her. I felt terrible, but the lying and cover-up about my addiction kept growing."

"Did she ever catch you?"

"One time she walked in on me when I was on a questionable Internet site. I exited the site quickly, but I think she saw. She didn't say anything, but I could see the disappointment in her eyes."

A few moments of silence passed. "So how has this affected your marriage?"

"It's been a disaster." A giant sigh. "She doesn't trust me. She's constantly interrogating me about what I've done or where I've been. I feel like I'm in jail. On top of that, it's ruined our sex life. I get greedy. She feels used. I can't get certain pictures out of my head. She feels inferior and inadequate. I get mad. She withdraws. I give up and decide to fulfill my fantasies without her. Then I feel guilty and ashamed." Trevor hid his face in his hands and mumbled, "This isn't the sort of husband I want to be."

Over the next few years, Julie discovered more and more about Trevor's secret battle. Meanwhile, Trevor got sucked deeper into porn until it was no longer satisfying by itself. He moved on to telephone sex and picking up women at bars. Every time Julie confronted him, he would beg for forgiveness. Julie was a compassionate person, but enough was enough. Even though she still loved him, she could not live like that. So she filed for divorce, took custody of their three grade-school children, and left the state.

The number of men who struggle with some form of sexual addiction would surprise most women. We live in an oversexualized culture that traps many men. I think sex is wonderful, but it has its appropriate and inappropriate expressions. Sex with one's spouse is the healthiest, most fulfilling type of sex. Porn twists something beautiful. Porn is not healthy, harmless, or innocent. It builds a wall between a husband and wife, no matter how much one or both may deny it. Porn undermines and often destroys a relationship. *There is absolutely no good excuse or justification for porn.* It's more dangerous than most men realize. Women intuitively recognize its danger, but in an attempt to be open-minded and nonjudgmental they often underrate their own good sense.

A man may have strong sexual desires, but these should be

directed only toward his wife—nobody else, fantasy or real. The wise Job wrote, "I made a covenant with my eyes not to look lustfully at a girl" (Job 31:1). Concerning a flirtatious stranger, Solomon counseled, "Do not lust in your heart after her beauty or let her captivate you with her eyes" (Proverbs 6:25). Even Jesus Himself said, "Anyone who looks at a woman lustfully has already committed adultery with her in his heart" (Matthew 5:28). Why do these three men make such an issue of the power of sexual imagery? Because it's so dangerous to one's marriage.

Whenever a man looks beyond his wife for any form of sexual arousal or fulfillment, he is setting himself up for trouble. Here are eight ways porn attacks a marriage.

1. It creates unrealistic and unsustainable visual, physical, and sexual expectations for one's marriage.

2. It focuses on personal gratification without nurturing a loving sensitivity toward one's wife.

3. It devalues the depth and power of sex by minimizing its spiritual, emotional, and relational aspects.

4. It objectifies women, seeing them as sexual commodities while ignoring the depth of their true identity and inner beauty.

5. It promotes addictive, escapist patterns, which create distance between a husband and wife.

6. It undermines the healthy sexual excitement, mystery, and satisfaction that should be a part of every person's marriage.

7. It breeds a wife's mistrust of her husband, increasing her insecurity about herself and the relationship.

8. It opens the doors to inappropriate sexual fantasies with real or imaginary partners, which may increase the chance of actual physical affairs.

If a man struggles and falls into this trap, he and his marriage will experience many, if not all, of these sad consequences. Porn takes a man's visual leanings and turns them against his marriage.

But a woman's emotional leanings can also be turned against her marriage. Romance novels, as well as many magazines and TV shows and movies, while definitely less dangerous than porn, are not as innocent as most women claim.

Women are drawn to emotional connections, and a good storyteller can make this connection. These stories set up unrealistic expectations in women. Few men can perform as romantically as these books portray, at least not consistently. Men have jobs to do and bills to pay. And they don't tend to think romantically without some help. Just as women don't look perfect, men don't act perfect. Romance novels and other similar media subconsciously create a dissatisfaction with a woman's husband and marriage. *Why can't he do that? Why doesn't he try this? I would love it if he were more romantic. If he really treasured me, he would say these sorts of things.*

Unrealistically romantic stories cause women to respect unknown fantasy men and even to develop cravings or bonds with them. Real-life men can't possibly compete with them. A woman can project those fantasy images onto a man to whom she's not married, opening the door to an emotional affair, which can develop into a sexual affair. In reality, affairs of any kind never work out as positively as one imagines.

Just as porn promotes inappropriate physical temptations, so romance novels and the like promote inappropriate emotional temptations. So why even go there? I'm not speaking against novels, movies, or TV shows that *include* romance; these can provide wonderful, relaxing interludes to life's stress. I'm speaking about those stories with a romantic intensity that's so absorbing it draws you into an emotional fantasy that is more attractive than real life.

Women must be very careful about those fantasies. But every husband should read at least one romance novel per year. Several years ago I read a powerful novel by a well-known, best-selling author. It was an incredible book about a husband fighting to save his marriage. But I don't want women to read it. No man can possibly be as amazingly romantic as the man in that book. But I want guys to use a man like that as an example to emulate. A nonerotic romance novel can do the following for an open-minded husband:

- Show him what emotionally impacts his wife.
- Give him a picture of her emotional world.
- Provide romantic ideas and strategies for him.
- Challenge him to reach out and touch her heart.

Romance should come from a woman's husband, if she's married, and no one and nothing else. Therefore husbands, filling a one-of-a-kind role, need to learn how to be much more romantic.

When it comes to intimate male-female connections, a husband and wife should lean on each other. For a man to meet his sexual needs, of any kind, outside the marriage is foolish and wrong. It shows a lack of character and commitment. Likewise, for a woman to meet her intimate emotional needs outside the marriage is equally foolish and wrong. A husband should look lovingly to his wife and only to his wife, while she should be available as much as she reasonably can. Meanwhile a wife should look lovingly to her husband and only to her husband, while he should be available as much as he reasonably can. I know this is idealistic and that many things can complicate this scenario. But it's still your only safe and healthy target.

Anything else is playing with fire.

CHAPTER SUMMARY

Porn is a serious danger to most men, implanting unrealistic visual and sexual expectations; romance novels and some movies and TV shows can also be risky for many women, implanting unrealistic romantic expectations.

1. How has porn been a struggle for him?
2. Which of the eight ways porn attacks a marriage (page 181) would your relationship be most susceptible to?
3. How have romance novels (or other types of romance media, like magazines, TV, or movies) presented a danger for her?

THIRTY-FIVE

Reach Out and Touch Someone

The world is full of lonely people. Just because people are married doesn't exempt them from feeling alone. We fill our lives with activities and stuff, but none of it shakes the feeling of abandonment.

Both men and women need closeness and intimacy. Men enjoy their independence and space, but there are crucial times when they yearn for connection. Men may pretend it's not important to them or that they don't have time for it. Yet as soon as a relationship falls apart, they ache like they never thought possible. Women are more continuously aware of this need. They think about it, read about it, talk about it. There's no way they'll forget it. They live for connection.

Once again, men and women prove how different they are. Though they both seek the same destination—intimacy—the routes they follow are miles apart. Women seek closeness through words; men seek closeness through touch.

Now, if some of the content of this chapter sounds similar to earlier chapters, that's by design. First, these issues are so central to understanding the differences between the genders that they bear repeated examination. Second, there's so much to say about men's and women's distinct strivings for intimacy that it can't all fit into one or even two chapters.

Both men and women feel an inner drive or compulsion to follow their pathways toward intimacy. To women, a lack of talk creates an internal emotional pressure that builds and builds, desperately craving release. In a similar way, to men, a lack of sex creates an internal physical pressure that builds and builds, desperately wanting release. Just as it's difficult for women to go more than two or three days without a meaningful verbal connection, so it's difficult for men to go more than two or three days without a meaningful sexual connection. Women may not need sex, and men may not need talk, but loving each other involves being attuned to our spouses' needs and doing all we can to meet them.

When you meet your spouse's needs, you're loving yourself too. There are few better ways for a woman to get her husband to talk than being sexually available. And men need to realize that the more a woman feels verbally connected to her husband, the more she draws emotionally close and opens her heart to sexual intimacy.

Positive talk helps a woman to feel more secure and confident. Silence frequently leaves a woman filling in the blanks with her greatest fears and worst-case scenarios. A man has incredible influence over the emotions and attitudes of his wife. What he says and how he says it can...

- calm her fears.
- boost her self-esteem.
- create a romantic mood.
- draw her close.
- prepare her for an intimate time.

Women want their husbands to talk without lecturing and listen without being passive. Smart men understand that good conversation can be the best foreplay.

When he tries verbally, she knows he cares. When she tries sexually, he knows she cares. A man feels closer to his wife when they are sexually connected. He also feels...

- more loved.
- more respected.
- more positive.
- more motivated.
- more generous.

Just as a woman needs consistent, regular communication with her husband, so a man needs consistent, regular sexual times with his wife. When these don't happen, except during times of mutual agreement, he feels rejected, insecure, or unimportant. He may try to make the most of it, but his irritability and isolation frequently grow. Most men are very hesitant to bring up their growing frustration because it makes them look needy or pathetic. One man told me, "I'm not going to beg. She knows my needs and how important this is to a healthy marriage. I just can't believe how mean and insensitive she can be by ignoring our sexual relationship. I thought she loved me."

When a man feels pushed away sexually, sooner or later he will withdraw into a state of hurt and resentment. Unfortunately this makes him susceptible to look places he has no business looking and to think things he shouldn't be thinking. During these times he is more vulnerable to inappropriate sexual temptations that he will later regret. Now, a wife is not responsible for her husband's sexual temptations or failures. This is a very important principle. Any man who blames his wife for his sexual struggles is out of line. Yet a wife has the power to make his struggle more difficult by staying unavailable. Most men assume that this lack of sexual availability is intentional and maybe even manipulative. How can she *not* be aware of how long it's been and how frustrated he's feeling? Men are often surprised to learn that women can actually forget about sex, and during periods of high stress or hectic activity it may be the last thing on their minds. For a long time. Likewise men might go days without even thinking about talking, unless they need something or are asked a question.

Touch is crucial to every marriage. Women enjoy nonsexual touch—holding hands, sitting close, an arm around her shoulder, a back rub, cuddling. This sort of touching is highly romantic and affirming to most women. Men might like nonsexual touching, but let's be honest—they like sexual touching a lot more. This is how they're built. But if they would take the time to provide loving, gentle nonsexual touch throughout the day, they might be surprised at their wives' resulting openness to more intimate touch in the evening. Women need to slow down and redirect their husbands' physical contact at times. But they need to be careful about belittling or humiliating him for sexual touching. After all, it is natural and wonderful. Meanwhile, men need to be more respectful about how, where, and when they touch. Random groping and grabbing without positive foreplay is offensive to most women. Husbands and wives need to accept and enjoy the wonders of touch. Stop complaining and start celebrating; God has given each of you to the other in spite of your differences.

Sexuality is incredibly powerful. It's not the solution to every problem, but it reminds a couple that they are a team and that they have a unique intimate connection they share with no one else. King Solomon wrote a whole book on this connection, titled Song of Songs. Here are a few of the principles:

1. Kiss again and again (1:2).
2. Retreat to the bedroom (1:4).

3. Be verbally romantic (1:15–16).
4. Touch each other (2:6).
5. Tell of your yearning (3:1).
6. Hold each other (3:4).
7. Get excited (5:4).
8. Give yourself fully (6:3).
9. Express your love (7:12).
10. Enjoy each other (8:10).

Take Solomon's suggestions and practice them regularly. They will improve your intimate times and increase your appreciation of your mate. In the sexual arena men and women operate so very differently, but that doesn't have to be a problem. It can be a part of the intrigue and adventure that enhance your relationship beyond your wildest dreams.

Every couple wants a better relationship. Women will say that the solution is to improve the communication. Men will say it's to improve the sex. And they're both absolutely right.

So both of you pitch in. Then nobody's lonely.

TRANSLATION GUIDE

Women: His desire for sex means "I long for intimacy with you, and I feel closest to you during sex."

Men: Her desire for talk means "I long for intimacy with you, and I feel closest to you through talk and nonsexual touch."

1. In what ways does communication open her heart?
2. In what ways does sexual connection open his heart?
3. Which of King Solomon's ten principles about intimacy (pages 188–189) are most important to you? Which are most important to your partner?

THIRTY-SIX

Why He Can't Ask for Directions

D o you know where we're going?" asked Nicole as Dean made a hesitant decision at yet another intersection.

"Of course I do," said Dean.

"Then why have we been driving for an hour when you said it would only take twenty minutes?"

"I guess it's farther than I thought."

"But isn't it south of Coyote Creek?"

"Yes," said Dean in frustration, "but I can't find Barton Road."

"Maybe we should stop at the next service station and ask?"

"No, I can figure this out. I think we're almost there."

"We're lost," Nicole declared.

"I don't think so. We just haven't figured out exactly where we are yet."

Nicole silently shook her head and smiled knowingly.

Sooner or later we all get lost.

Admitting that they are lost is much tougher for men than for women. It involves publicly confessing that they made a mistake and aren't sure what they're doing. To most men, getting lost is a sign of failure. To most women, getting lost is simply a part of everyday life. If they make a mistake, so be it. Welcome to the human race. Everybody makes mistakes. But for men, being lost is a problem—a problem they have to fix. Without help.

Men are independent, or at least they believe they should be. To ask for directions or help of any kind is a sign of dependency. Women recognize that at various times we are all dependent. To deny this seems irrational to most women, but to admit it seems weak to most men. To men, asking for help feels as if they are putting themselves in a one-down position, which is incredibly humiliating. Yet men feel honor bound to respond to someone else's request for help.

Women may even enjoy asking for help. Seeking assistance of any kind provides an opportunity for connections—verbal, emotional, relational connections. But to a man, talking about his problems seems negative, bordering on complaining. Men are private with their troubles; women are public with them. Men minimize their problems and try to figure out how to fix them on their own. Anything else feels like an embarrassing failure.

Men only share a problem if they are stuck and don't know how to fix it themselves. Women frequently share a problem to provide a reason to interact with their husbands. But husbands honestly believe that their wives simply want the problem fixed, so they offer the simplest, quickest fixes possible. Yet most of the time women don't want it fixed; they want their husbands to listen. If a husband isn't sure what she wants, he should ask, "Do you want me to fix it or just listen?" Then a smart man will give her what *she says* she needs, not what *he thinks* she needs.

Now, getting back to why he won't ask for directions… Sure, he's independent and wants to solve this problem himself, but there are other reasons. Men are visual-spatial thinkers. They tend to be better at navigating a route than women. They orient themselves by the lay of the land and visual markers. Men like maps; they show the big picture. With a map men can chart out their course before a trip. Then if something goes wrong, they can return to the map and figure out where they got off course. When a man has a map, he doesn't need anybody's help. Even if a man doesn't have a physical map, he often has a mental map to orient himself.

Women are more verbal and less visual in orienting themselves. They create a verbal sequence that gets them from point A to point B. When women get off their verbal sequence and see no familiar landmark to reorient themselves, they know they're lost. When men are lost, it feels like a temporary state, which pushes them to their visual or mental map. Being lost becomes a challenge to their problem-solving skills. It's something to overcome and conquer. When women are lost, it feels like a permanent state, which can only be solved by seeking outside help. So the most logical solution for women is to seek verbal directions. This solution seems so quick and easy that it perplexes most women when their husbands don't immediately accept it. Yet verbal directions are not always as helpful to men. When a man hears verbal directions, he may end up more confused because he doesn't naturally orient himself verbally. In fact, those words may overwhelm him and make him more lost. He needs visual-spatial orientation, not verbal orientation. Men ask for directions as a last resort, when all else has failed.

Life is rarely as straightforward as we would like. We all need help. We all need directions. But we're all different. Men need to figure it out themselves. Women need verbal confirmation and interaction. How do we respect these differences without letting them drive us crazy or make us hostile toward each other? Bottom line: men sometimes need to swallow their pride and just ask for directions. And women sometimes need to be more patient and just let men figure it out themselves.

In other words, *let men be men and women be women.*

TRANSLATION GUIDE

Women: His resistance to verbal direction or help really means "I solve problems spatially, and words sometimes just confuse me more; I also thrive on 'winning' when I figure it out myself."

Men: Her desire for verbal direction and help means "I solve problems verbally, and I also need the social connection that talking provides."

1. Men, what does it mean to you when you must ask for directions? How often and under what circumstances do you ask?
2. Women, what does it mean to you when you must ask for directions?
3. How do each of you find your way around an unfamiliar area?

THIRTY-SEVEN

As Close as the East Is to the West

This just isn't fair." Tami glared at me.

In my most mature, well-educated fashion, I glared back.

"If we both love each other so much," she continued, "why does this have to be so hard?"

"There has to be a good compromise," I reasoned. "We just have to keep looking."

"But we've been looking for two full months." She was working hard to stay calm. "All I want is a couch for our family room. I'm tired of sitting on the floor."

Tami is an excellent interior decorator. But the casual blue denim couch she'd fallen in love with just didn't fit my taste. Tami had come up with a well-thought-out plan for redecorating our drab-looking family room, and she was excited about it. New curtains, new carpet, new paint, new easy chair.

New blue denim couch.

I felt great with all of her decisions. Except the last one. I thought the fact that we had agreed on so much was a miracle. Ever since Tami and I were first married, we knew that our tastes in decorating were diametrically opposed. She liked knickknacks; I liked sparseness. She liked colorful walls; I liked white. She liked more contemporary; I liked more traditional. At times we had a hard time agreeing. In fact, it took us seven years to concur on a painting for our bedroom. So it was no surprise that we didn't see eye to eye on a couch.

"Isn't this cute?" Tami had smiled coyly as she lounged on the blue denim couch at the furniture store.

I hesitated and considered how honest I should be. But before I could say anything, she declared, "It's absolutely perfect. It's exactly what I've been hoping to find. What do you think?"

"Well, since you asked," I blurted, "I think it's ugly."

The showroom went silent. Tami's countenance dropped.

"But don't worry," I said optimistically. "Let's go to another store. There are a lot of places in town; I'm sure we can find something we both like."

Another two months passed, and we visited every furniture showroom within a twenty-mile radius. That's a lot of stores. But I couldn't find anything that would distract her from the blue denim couch. "Are you sure there isn't anything else you'd be content with?" I asked in desperation.

"Nothing I've seen yet," she said, a little too confidently.

I'd given it my best try, but we were stuck. Our different tastes had arrived at a standoff. I had a choice. I could dig in my heels and stand my ground. Or I could let it go and show Tami that her happiness was more important than my preference. "Can I think about it for a few minutes?" I asked. She consented, and I went outside to get some space and clear my head.

Tami was ecstatic when, later that week, the blue denim couch was delivered. Finally she was able to complete the redecoration of our family room.

———————

Over time the couch has grown on me. It's comfortable and cozy. It fits well with Tami's new color scheme. Even though it's not my taste, I've truly come to like it.

That's how it frequently is with differences. You start out resistant, but then soften. In the end you learn to appreciate and enjoy the differences.

Opposites attract. And once they marry, they often drive each other crazy. Every person is an individual. Unique. One of a kind. Every couple has their share of differences. Some of these are related to gender, but many are the result of two distinct personalities trying to live together and interface their individual preferences. Personality differences are rarely an issue of right and wrong. They're simply differences. Tami likes cats; I don't. I like biking; she doesn't. She likes the house warm, and I like it cool. I like the city, and she likes the country. We like different music, different art, different TV shows. Our differences are sometimes frustrating. But they can also be fascinating. They pull us from our comfortable ruts and stretch us beyond our narrow perspectives, exposing us to new, fresh horizons. Differences add variety and depth and opportunities for growth. They make us more complete. As I understand and learn to appreciate Tami's preferences, I draw closer to her, and our marriage grows richer.

Here are seven common differences that frequently show up in a marriage. They have nothing to do with gender, but that doesn't keep them from starting plenty of conflicts between husband and wife.

Extroverts and Introverts. Extroverts love crowds—the more people, the merrier. They're energized by people. Introverts would rather spend the evening in solitude or with a few close friends. They might enjoy people, but too much time with others can wear them out.

Leapers and Lookers. Leapers take risks. When they see an opportunity, they jump on it quickly, before it's too late. Lookers are more cautious. Before making decisions, they gather information, analyze, ponder, consider options, question, evaluate consequences, pray. Then they may do it all over again, just in case they forgot something.

Spenders and Savers. If spenders have money, they want to unload it as quickly as possible, grabbing at every spending opportunity. Savers hesitate to spend any more than absolutely necessary. They love to save, for one never knows when you might need that extra money.

Runners and Relaxers. Runners are always busy. They're on the move from dawn to dusk, constantly racing from one point to the next. Relaxers like to take their time, catch their breath, play a little, enjoy the moment. They sit back and don't let others push them.

Dreamers and Drivers. Dreamers are visionaries who love to come up with creative ideas. Dreamers are optimists who believe anything is possible, and they always have new ideas to make it happen. Drivers are practical, hands-on, hard workers. They're frequently seen as pessimistic, but they're the ones who turn the dreams into reality.

Collectors and Tossers. Collectors gather things. They hate to throw anything away; they might need it as soon as it's gone. Tossers love to get rid of things. If something hasn't been used in the past year, tossers get rid of it. They see the collector's treasure as clutter.

Planners and Flexers. Planners love structure and schedules. They want everything logically organized and neatly packaged. They believe everything has its proper time and place. Flexers bend with the flow of life. They are more spontaneous and organic, sometimes even random. They feel fine with loose ends.

It's surprising to me that most couples are opposites in at least half of the seven areas in this list. (I'll let you decide how to divide seven in half.)

Most couples have little understanding and almost no tolerance for differences. We all want our spouses to think and act like we do. So we begin a subtle and sometimes not-so-subtle process of trying to convert our spouses to "the right way" or "the best way." Which, of course, is "my way." I've tried this for years with Tami, but she just won't budge. In fact, she has the gall to try converting me to her way. The reality is that her way is just as valid and right as my way.

Differences are not only normal and healthy—they're crucially important for a healthy marriage. Differences are a wonderful strength. They provide balance and open one's eyes to varied perspectives. Above everything else, differences give me opportunities to love Tami for who she is. They challenge me to reach beyond my selfishness, my preferences, and my way, to show her a humble, unconditional, generous love. The apostle Peter wrote, "Above all, love each other deeply, because love covers over a multitude of sins" (1 Peter 4:8). I need to work harder to show Tami this kind of deep love. After all, this relationship isn't just about me—it's about us.

As I write these words, I'm sitting on our blue denim couch. I'm not sure why I was so resistant to getting it. It looks great in our family room. Tami just sat down beside me and snuggled close. I slip my arm around her and say, "I sure do love you."

"Now what made you say that?" she asks.

"I was just thinking about what great taste you have and how much I like this couch."

"Really?" she says in shock.

"Really." I kiss her on the forehead, and we wrap our arms around each other.

CHAPTER SUMMARY

Every couple has their share of nongender differences involving taste, preferences, personality, style of life, and many other factors. When you value these differences, they become strengths in the relationship.

1. How do the two of you resolve differences of taste?
2. Of the seven common differences on pages 197–198, which ones characterize the two of you?
3. How have your personality differences made you stronger and better as a couple?

THIRTY-EIGHT

Linguistics of Love

M en have bigger brains.

But women have more brain cells.

Neither is better; they're just different. But we tend to reject and put down what we don't understand. Often, men don't make sense to women, and women don't make sense to men. Men wish women would think and feel and act like them, while women wish the same thing (uh, the other way around, I mean). But men are men. And women are women. That's just the way it is.

Men and women spend far too much time complaining about these differences and far too little time trying to understand them.

God made men and women different for good reason. The genders complement each other intriguingly, and that can strengthen our relationships...if we let it. We need to relax and enjoy the differences. They provide opportunities for us to grow and mature. It's in maturity that we move beyond personal comfort and preference. It's in maturity that we love our partners more than ourselves. It's in maturity that we accept and appreciate our spouses as God's amazing gifts to us.

Every difference has its positive side. We don't need to fight them; they have much to teach us. Differences are best celebrated, not condemned. Instead of ignoring or minimizing our differences, husbands and wives need to maximize them. For each of the differences we've examined, we should each compliment and thank our spouses. I'm so glad Tami isn't just like me. Even though I sometimes complain, I wouldn't have her any other way. Her special qualities cause me to love her all the more. They don't always make life easier, but they make it better.

Differences challenge our patience, our compassion, our understanding, our humility. We sometimes resent differences because they spotlight three embarrassing weaknesses, with which we all periodically struggle:

Confusion. I don't understand why my spouse is doing what he or she is doing.

Selfishness. I want things to go my way, bending life to my wishes.

Stubbornness. I will fight and belittle all that doesn't succumb to my plans.

The best marriages know how to reduce these three conditions. They replace confusion with patient attempts to understand, selfishness with generous compassion, and stubbornness with gentle, humble flexibility. As we let go of these three negatives and replace them with their positive counterparts, the reasons for fighting over our differences fade away.

So what do we do with all our differences? How do we keep them from pulling us apart? There are at least four strategies we can use. Each individual difference may call for a different strategy. Here are the ABCs (and D) of making the most of our uniquenesses:

Accept. Sometimes we just need to relax and accept the situation the way it is. He is the way he is; she is the way she is. Things aren't going to change, and that's okay. Everything doesn't have to go our way.

Back down. Sometimes we need to admit that our spouses have good points, and their way might even be better than our way. Then we back down and make the changes they prefer, without complaining or copping an attitude.

Compromise. In certain situations we both need to look for the middle ground and find a compromise the two of us can live with. A healthy compromise—both spouses willing to change—can be a strong statement of mutual respect.

Discuss. If the previous three strategies don't work, this is the last option. We discuss—not demand—whether the other spouse is willing to make a change. We humbly explain why this is important to us and graciously accept their decision.

The best marriages tend to manage differences by using a combination of all four strategies.

Now, it's important to note that the two sexes are actually more alike than they are different. The differences stand out, but the similarities help us to relax and identify with each other. Tami and I have hundreds of similarities. We share a common faith, a commitment to growth, a compassion for others. We both enjoy books and sunsets and traveling to sunny getaways. We love walks on the beach and Chinese food and our three incredible children. The list is endless. Our differences may give us depth, but our similarities bring us bonding. The longer we're married, the more our differences find peace with each other and the more similarities we seem to discover.

We've discovered a basic formula that can improve and strengthen any marriage. It's incredibly simple and surprisingly effective. *Take the time to know your spouse's needs, and do all you possibly can to meet those needs.* If every husband and wife would seriously work at this, it would revolutionize marriages. Divorce rates would drop; love and respect would soar. We need to stop thinking about what's fair. We need to start reflecting on what's healthy and healing and helpful. If we would only put our spouses' needs first, in most situations they would return the favor. Mutually meeting each other's needs is a sign of a mature relationship. I love situations where Tami and I both are satisfied. It feels great when both husband and wife win.

It's Friday afternoon, and I have the rest of my day planned. I'm in my project box—I need to change the oil in my car, mow my lawn, return a bulging inbox of e-mail, and finish the last chapter of this book. My time is packed, but then I reread the words I just wrote about meeting each other's needs. Suddenly I feel a pang of conviction. I hate it when this happens. It's one thing when they're someone else's words, but when your own words smack you on the side of the head, it really hurts.

Several months ago, Tami told me that one of her favorite things to do is to get away from the kids on a Friday afternoon and go to Stanford's, a cozy little restaurant down the road. She loves to snuggle into a booth with an appetizer and a cup of hot tea. Here she unwinds and talks about her week—conversation and connection. If I was a good husband, I'd call her right now and ask her to meet me there. But I don't want to go there. I need some space and independence. I don't want to talk. I want to get things done so I can check them off my list.

A good husband would do what you tell other guys to do. And you probably wouldn't even give it a second thought.

So here's the test. Do I listen to my own words, or do I stay on task and finish my projects?

I pick up the phone and call. "Hey, Tami, would you like to go out to Stanford's?"

"Oh, that would be wonderful." I hear her smiling.

"I'll meet you there in fifteen minutes."

"I'll be there."

I'm glad I asked. If I'm thinking about her needs, no matter how different, it's easy to get on the same page. If I love, she'll love. If I give, she'll give. If I stretch beyond my confusion and selfishness and stubbornness, so will she.

Marriage is tough sometimes. But give it a little effort. None of us needs to be lost in translation.

CHAPTER SUMMARY

Every difference has a positive resolution that can make your relationship stronger and deeper.

1. What challenges arise from your differences?
2. When was the last time you fought about any of the differences discussed in this book? How was that fight resolved?
3. Which of the ABCs (and D) of coping do you find easiest and hardest for her? for him? for both of you as a couple?

FRIENDLY REMINDERS

There are times we are all lost in translation, and hopefully you've found some of the insights in this book helpful. Here are some final questions for every couple to ask each other. They will help you get closer, go deeper, understand more, and build a relationship that can last a lifetime.

Please photocopy these questions and put them in your purse, in your wallet, in your appointment book, in your desk drawer, on your mirror, on your refrigerator, or wherever you'll have ready access to them on a regular basis.

Then decide how you want to use them. You might…

- Review the whole list once a week.
- Read one or two points each day (or each week).
- Use them whenever your relationship isn't exactly where you want it to be.
- Scan through the list until a pertinent question jumps out at you.
- Use them to guide periodic evaluative discussions as a couple.

However you choose to use these questions, let them be a tool to improve yourself and your relationship. Let each question teach you and remind you and challenge you. Let this list be a starting gun to motivate you and a mirror to show you how you are doing. But let them also direct you to love your mate in ways he or she will never forget.

So here we go with The Questions:

1. Have you taken an opportunity to express your love today?
2. Are you letting a difference become a problem when it doesn't have to be?
3. Is it time to do something his or her way instead of your way?

4. Is there some difficulty that you need help or encouragement for? Or that your spouse needs help and encouragement for?

5. Have you truly listened to your spouse today?

6. Does your balance between space and closeness need any adjusting?

7. Do you have a need your spouse might not be aware of? Is he or she exhibiting some behavior that might reflect a need you don't know about?

8. What is one way you can build quality time into the next day or two so you can both really connect?

9. Is there something for which you need to say "I'm sorry"?

10. Are you holding on to something negative that you need to let go of?

11. What's one way you can surprise your spouse with a compliment or a gift?

12. Have you been focused more on giving than on taking?

13. What's one way you can actively show love and respect today?

14. Has an issue arisen on which it would be better to remain quiet?

15. What's something you can do to maintain your positive sexual relationship?

16. Have you *not* shown your love recently because you didn't feel like it? What's one way you can show it anyway?

17. What's one passing annoyance or difference that you need to release to keep it from turning into a conflict?

18. What's one way you can celebrate your similarities and differences today?

19. When was the last time you reaffirmed your commitment to love and cherish your spouse for "as long as you both shall live"? Is it time to reaffirm it today?

20. Have you thanked God for your spouse today?

Acknowledgments

We are all influenced, impacted, and inspired by hundreds of people who intersect with our lives. None of us works or lives in a vacuum. None of us can do it alone. This book is no exception, for it was built on the professional work, research, writings, and presentations of many wonderful people. Some of these are: Dave and Claudia Arp, Dr. James Dobson, Dr. Emerson Eggerichs, Bill and Pam Farrel, Jeff and Shaunti Feldhahn, Dr. John Gottman, Dr. John Gray, Dr. Willard Harley, Dr. Kevin Leman, Dr. Patricia Love, Dr. Gary and Barbara Rosberg, Dr. Laura Schlessinger, Dr. Steven Stosny, and Dr. Deborah Tannen. There are probably many more who have influenced this book, and I apologize for their names not being included.

I would also like to thank the great team at Multnomah, who believed in this project with a passion before a word was ever written. Their encouragement and excitement were fantastic. So a special thanks is deserved by Brian Smith, Kimberly Brock, Guy Coleman, Doug Gabbert, and all the others who made this happen.

I'd also like to thank all those individuals and couples who read the early drafts of the manuscript and gave me their honest feedback: Dr. Carol Clifton, Doug and Diane Crosby, Steve and Ann Liday, Todd and Monica Powers, Dan and Shani Roe, Bill and Denease Schmidt, David and Sarah Van Diest, Paul and April Waggoner.

An extra special thanks goes to Keely Hannon, my wonderful assistant, who keeps my office organized and my schedule straight. She encouraged me at each step of this project, cheering me forward and turning my scribbled thoughts into a readable manuscript.

Lastly, and most importantly, is my dear Tami, who is the best wife any man could ever wish for. I'm sorry all these differences sometimes drive you crazy. Thank you for living this book with me. Hopefully I'll take my own words seriously, and this book will help me be a better husband.

BRAVE MEN BEAR REAL WOUNDS

Beneath a man's armor, they may be bloodied, beaten, or broken. Where there was once courage and confidence, they now harbor heartache and pain. Life—in all its glory—has taken its toll.

But this is not the end. It is where healing starts and life begins. Dr. Steve Stephens speaks man-to-man about all kinds of wounds from the subtle burden of living with nagging regrets, to gut-wrenching blows.

More than encouragement and guidance, *The Wounded Warrior* is packed with pointed questions, scriptural teachings, and honest talk about practical solutions for men.

Available in bookstores and from online retailers.

MULTNOMAH BOOKS
www.mpbooks.com

Check out
these other titles

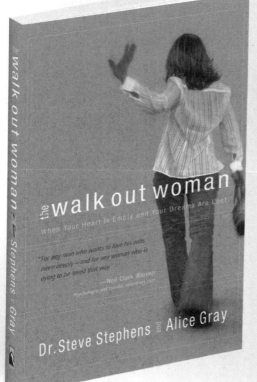

The Walk Out Woman
When Your Heart is Empty and Your Dreams Are Lost

There is an epidemic of women walking out on their marriages today. In *The Walk Out Woman*, Dr. Steve Stephens and Alice Gray bring you practical solutions to heal your relationship.

from
Dr. Steve Stephens:

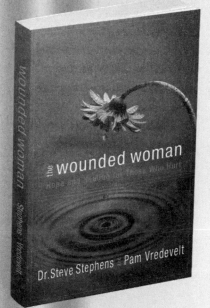

The Wounded Woman
Hope and Healing for Those Who Hurt

It's your turn to live the good life! This book is every woman's tool for releasing the hurts that hinder and moving forward to your glorious, liberated future!

The Worn Out Woman
When Life Is Full and Your Spirit Is Empty

Are you full or empty? Energized or exhausted? Focused or distracted? Everyone has a breaking point—and you may be closer to yours than you realize. Here's help.